C000005825

A
Doctor's
Tale

To

Trevor & Gillian

with

Best Wishes

A Doctor's Tale

Joshua Gerwyn Elias

First impression: 2010

© Copyright Joshua Gerwyn Elias and Y Lolfa Cyf., 2010

The contents of this book are subject to copyright, and may
not be reproduced by any means, mechanical or electronic,
without the prior, written consent of the publishers.

Cover design: Y Lolfa

ISBN: 978 184771 306 3

Published, printed and bound in Wales
by Y Lolfa Cyf., Talybont, Ceredigion SY24 5HE
website www.ylolfa.com
e-mail ylolfa@ylolfa.com
tel 01970 832 304
fax 832 782

THE START OF THE JOURNEY

I WAS ONLY TWO years old when the accident happened that affected me for the rest of my life.

My mother, Ray, was one of seven children and came from the Cilie family of poets in Cardiganshire. My father, Illtud, was also a Cardiganshire man, one of twelve children from Glanhirwen, a smallholding near Beulah. He went to sea as a deck hand at the age of fifteen and sailed from Barry. He had a hard life and told us many interesting stories of his life on board cargo ships.

After they were married my parents both worked on a milk round in Bristol. The milk would arrive in large tankers from the farms and had to be bottled and distributed to the houses. The work did not finish there – empty bottles had to be washed and prepared for the next day. It was a busy time!

My mother always used to bathe my younger brother, Hefin, and me in a zinc bath on the hearth. She used to put the boiling water in first and then the cold water, but one day, before she had time to add the cold water, I jumped into the bath thinking it was ready. My injuries were horrific – severe burns, especially to the buttocks and legs, and I was rushed to the Bristol Royal Infirmary. At the hospital, the blisters and scalded skin were treated. The experience was so frightening that I cannot remember the incident or the hospital. Nature has kindly blotted it all from my memory.

However, when I left hospital my speech was badly affected, and since then, I have suffered from a severe stammer. The boy who had been a chatterbox suddenly had great difficulty in speaking. Shock was mainly responsible for my condition, but on top of the shock was the trauma of being alone in hospital without my family. Today, parents are allowed to stay as long as they like, even sleeping nearby if necessary. At that time, only an hour a day was allowed for visiting. Doctors now realise how important it is for the child not to be completely cut off from his parents for a long time. Three things are necessary to ensure the psychological well being of a child in hospital as well as at home: love, affection and security. If the child gets all three, he has a better chance of returning to full health quickly.

In 1938, shortly before the war, my parents moved to Haverfordwest, where my father found a job as a petrol lorry driver. I attended the primary school at Prendergast, and before long my brother Hefin joined me there when he was four; by then I was six. I considered it to be my job to look after him. One day in the playground, one of the bullies punched him. Seeing this happen, my reaction was to do the same to him!

I attended Fenton School and used to walk home for lunch, some 300 yards away. One day, I suffered another traumatic experience. I was walking on my own back to school carrying a bag full of old clothes that were being collected to help the war effort.

Fifty yards from the school, I heard the sound of an aeroplane and looked up to see a German bomber, with Swastikas painted on both wings. Within seconds, it dropped two bombs that exploded with a bang like a thunderclap, with dust rising several metres into the air. The air-raid siren could soon be heard, but by then the aeroplane had disappeared over the horizon.

It was a frightful experience and I ran as fast as I could to school, where the children were crying hysterically and the teachers trying to calm and comfort them. These bombs killed nobody, but the next day, a German bomber returned to almost the same place, and dropped more bombs and two adults lost their lives. To a boy of six, of a nervous disposition and suffering from a severe stammer, it was another traumatic experience.

After the bombing, my mother, who feared for our lives, insisted, like a hen shielding her chicks under her wings, that she would take us to a place where we would be safe. This meant taking my brother and myself 'to the country'. She took us to an area on the Cardiganshire coast that she knew well, where she had lived during her youth. My father stayed in Haverfordwest to work. We found refuge in an old cottage about half a mile from the seaside at Cwmtydu.

My grandmother Esther came from a family of poets and one of her brothers, John, emigrated to Canada in 1904. His most famous lines are carved around the entrance door to the memorial chamber of the parliament buildings in Ottawa. 'All's well, for over there among his peers a Happy Warrior sleeps.'

John, known as 'Jac Canada' described Cwmtydu in a romantic manner:

> Home of the bard and the Cardi – a mint
> Of romance and beauty
> A village in the valley
> Smiling by the surging sea.
>
> Leisure in deep seclusion – far away
> From the world's mad passion
> In this great isolation
> I would live and die alone

As wartime evacuees our life was less idyllic and much harsher than that romantic picture of Cwmtydu. The house, Penplas, was not your ideal cottage with a thatched roof. The cottage itself was in a bad state of repair and its roof was covered in rusting corrugated zinc. It had only two small dark musty rooms. One room was our bedroom and the other was used as a kitchen and living room. The toilet was a bucket in a rickety shed that was attached to the cottage. Luckily, there were woods nearby and my brother and I collected firewood to keep us warm on the cold winter nights. The old cottage is now a ruin. But we children loved the place and spent our days on the beach that was only some four hundred yards away.

To me, Cwmtydu is the loveliest cove on the whole of the Welsh coastline. It is a secluded bay that breaks the rugged coastline. Overlooked by grassy slopes, it has a shingle beach, with a small river named Ffynnon Dewi entering the sea at this point. The quiet six-mile stretch of coastline between New Quay to the north and Llangrannog, some two miles to the south, once provided an ideal setting for smuggling – mostly brandy from Ireland and France. The contraband was hidden in secluded caves until it could be safely carried inland on horseback. A notorious smuggler who used Cwmtydu cove was Twm Siôn Cwilt, named after his colourful patchwork coat. Travelling by night, he managed to avoid capture by the excisemen on several occasions and mystery surrounds his true identity.

Llangrannog and New Quay are both seaside resorts of immense beauty. Llangrannog was where Sir Edward Elgar spent many a summer holiday. He lived most of his life in the Welsh border country and spent his vacations in small seaside resorts on Cardigan Bay, where he found inspiration, using themes from some of the Welsh folk songs and hymn tunes he heard in his work. He suffered from bouts of depression, and this is when his friend Rose Burley came to his aid. She invited him and his wife Alice to stay at her rented house near the beach at Llangrannog, yards from the sea and next to the famous local, the Pentre Arms, owned for many years by Tom, my grandmother's brother. He also stayed at Baywell House and at Lochtyn Farm that was situated high above the bay.

One day on his way down to the beach from the farm on a well-trodden path he heard a male voice choir singing a Welsh hymn in a cave beneath the cliff, to the tune of 'Tanymarian'. He was inspired by the hymn and he used the theme for his introduction and *Allegro for Strings*. The choir was a group of men from the woollen mills of the Teifi valley who had been told by their family doctor that their coughing was due to inhaling wool fibre and that a day by the seaside would rid them of their malady.

My most vivid memory of the cottage at Cwmtydu during the war is of the white barn owl. At dusk, it could be seen hunting, looking for mice and voles. The pleasures of this idyllic paradise prevented me from responding to my mother's calls to come in to the house to prepare for bed. On hearing the owl hooting, she would say that if I did not come in the owl would attack me and take my eyes out. I remained frightened of this most beautiful of birds for years. In later years when I was studying child psychology, using this type of threat to make a child obedient was very much frowned upon.

It was in Haverfordwest that my twin brother and sister were born, Dyfed and Dilys. The GP had not diagnosed twins, and the midwife was alone when coping with a home delivery. Dilys weighed 8 lbs, Dyfed 7 lbs – the third heaviest twins born in Great Britain since records began.

After the twins were born, my mother needed help. This was provided by my aunt, Myfanwy Husak, who was a nurse in London and worked there throughout the Blitz. Her ability and experience to make sure a child looked at his or her best became obvious in a baby show in Clarbeston Road. Mother wanted me to compete in the open section, under five years of age. I was bathed, Vaseline put on my naturally curly hair and dressed in a new bathing suit. The judge was a doctor from Haverfordwest and he awarded me the Champion of the Show – out of fifty-two competitors. 'A perfect child' was his comment to my mother! Indeed, the family scooped all the prizes. Dilys and Dyfed for the best twins and Dyfed for the prettiest baby!

It was about this time that we made our visits to see my mam-gu, Esther. She was a delightful person, and her welcome always warm. My clearest memory is of her coming downstairs, facing backwards – I think this was because she was frightened of falling forwards on the stairs. She taught me a prayer to be recited every night at bedtime, in Welsh of course, translated roughly as follows:

I rest my head on the pillow to sleep,
I give myself to Christ,
If I die before the morn
May He keep my soul in heaven.

Her oatcakes were delicious, and watching her make them was a major part of the stay. Out came the basin, oat flour, sugar and melted butter, all mixed by hand. Then a rolling pin and, lastly, a teacup to shape the rounded cakes. They were placed on the bake stone and eaten while still warm with butter or cheese. It was a feast, and if my brother and mother were there, the last one would be devoured almost before she cooked it.

Soon my life was to change dramatically because of a childhood experience that was to prove even more damaging and traumatic than being scalded by boiling water, and which left mental scars that have remained with me to this day.

LOSING MY FAMILY – THE FOSTER CHILD

S OON AFTER THE TWINS were born I was torn from my family at the tender age of six years to be fostered. This experience was the darkest period in my life and caused such trauma that I have suffered all my life from its effects. My father came from the Elias family in Beulah near Newcastle Emlyn. His father, Jack, was a builder and very dexterous. Jack played the accordion in his spare time and would perform in local concerts. Sarah, his wife, was gentle and quiet. I remember the signs of hard work on her hands after raising twelve children. After the twins were born my parents struggled to cope with four children, all of a young age, and they turned to the Elias family for help.

Sarah had a sister, Lisa, who lived with her husband Evan at Alltycnydau farm, Croeslan near Llandysul. It was decided, after the problems in Haverfordwest with the bombing and my stammer that I would go to live with them. This was not unusual as fostering with relatives was common practice in Wales at that time.

Leaving my family was a heart-breaking experience. I would cry myself to sleep many a night. The experience had a profound psychological effect on me, and I can quite honestly say that I have spent my whole life trying to come to terms with what happened to me.

I know that it had an effect on my brother Hefin also. After I had left home for my new foster home, Hefin would ask my mother every day when would I be coming back. She would say, "Perhaps he will come on the bus tomorrow," knowing full well that I would not be there. Poor Hefin would go and wait for the bus every day for weeks in vain. He was hurt by my absence and missed my company; for years he would find a quiet hidden corner where he could cry without anybody seeing him.

I don't remember the first journey to the farm when I

was left there, and I don't remember how long it was before my parents came to see me from Haverfordwest. But I do remember, as if it were yesterday, them leaving the farm on their way home. I ran crying after the car for a quarter of a mile before I came to the end of the farm lane.

Alltycnydau Farm consisted of a stone-built house, with 80 acres of land, some of which was on a steep slope and difficult to manage, hence the name which means 'hillcrops'. Facilities in the house were basic, with no bath or toilet, like most farmhouses at that time. The toilet was outside the house, some ten yards away and built of corrugated zinc. Inside was a comfortable wooden toilet seat and a hole, probably six feet deep, which was never emptied and the toilet paper was the *Woman's Weekly* hanging on a nail! There was no lock on the door so on hearing someone approaching it was advisable to whistle or sing!

To the south of the farmyard, trees had been planted for shelter from the prevailing wind. The cowshed, stables and outhouses were the other side, with the pigsty, garden and rickyard further away. The buildings were on a slope, facing south, and were hot in summer and mild in the winter.

Water was a problem. The mains supply had not reached outlying farms, so we had to carry what was needed for drinking, washing, etc. from a source on our land, 200 yards away. There was no well, it just poured out of the ground near a large hole, about two feet in diameter.

The main source of income was milk, which was sold in bottles and distributed to the village of Croeslan and the surrounding area. What was left over went in churns to the Milk Marketing Board (MMB), with payment in the form of a cheque every month. Without this income we would have been poor even though we sold eggs, chickens, geese and turkeys at Christmas, the occasional horse or cow, and also potatoes.

During the war, the black market came into its own, and farmers sold eggs and butter illegally – foods that the government was rationing. A van used to arrive every Friday evening at the farm, driven by Mr Thomas, a butcher from Skewen, south Wales. He would fill the van with meat of all kinds, eggs and anything else he could sell in his shop. He would leave the farm after it was dark so that he would not be seen and caught. He covered the car's lights so that only a small hole would allow light to illuminate the road. This was to prevent any German aeroplanes seeing him from the air and attacking or bombing him!

Travelling over the bridge in Carmarthen one night, with his van full of food for the black market, he was stopped by a policeman. "What have you got in the back of the van?" asked the PC. Thomas pulled out a chicken from the back of the van and placed it in the policeman's hands whose next words were "Off you go"!

Like so much of Cardiganshire, the land was barren and stony, especially the fields on high ground. I can remember spending whole days collecting stones of all sizes and putting them in mounds, which were then collected by the cart, pulled by a horse and emptied into a quarry. Because the soil was so poor, it had to be enriched, and this was provided by the natural product from the animals on the farm – cow dung!

At the lower end of the farmyard was the dung heap, which had been emptied from the cowshed, stable, pigsty, etc. – even potato peelings from the kitchen – and left to rot. It provided excellent manure when carted to the fields and garden in the spring. The young cattle were kept indoors through the winter, and fresh straw was added daily to their bedding, reaching three or four feet high. I did my share, sometimes spending a week with my uncle and the farm servant clearing these winter quarters. No wonder I eventually left for university!

No machine could get to the steep fields at the bottom end of the farm that were often covered with ferns that chocked the grass. I can remember cutting the ferns with a scythe every year. The rabbits loved this wilderness and provided tasty meals before the days of myxomatosis.

Maybe the reason why the Cardis, like the Scots, are described as mean people is that the soil is so poor that there is so much hard work to make it fertile. To get a living from a farm in this area meant so much more work than areas like the Towy valley or Hereford and Worcester. Having worked so hard to earn the pennies, one did not want to spend or give them away. The only charity in Cardiganshire was the Cardi's pocket!

My Uncle Evan and Aunty Lisa were about 50 years old when they fostered me. Aunty Lisa was a workaholic who worked ceaselessly without ever taking a break. If she had a spare minute she made quilts. She had learnt the craft of quilting at Y Felin (The Mill), Llangrannog where she worked for three years. I still use Aunty Lisa's quilts – they are now 100 years old and none the worse for wear.

Uncle Evan was born and brought up at the farm during a very difficult time. His father had died when he was a year old, and had three sisters who were 2, 3 and 4 years old. He knew poverty and hardship. Work was his life and hobby. He knew little else, but could just write his name.

When I was 12 years old, he asked me to help him cut down an old oak tree in the valley to use as firewood during the winter. After sawing, it became obvious that the centre of the trunk was rotten. I will always remember his next words. He told me that there are three things that are difficult to know in life. In Welsh, they all start with 'd': 'dyn', 'derwen' and 'diwrnod' – a man, an oak tree and a day. Man can be deceitful, the tree can be rotten on the inside and a day can be sunny but soon turn to rain.

Uncle Evan went to chapel every Sunday. Religion was close to his heart, and he would not allow me to chop firewood or whistle on the Sabbath. He never took part in a service, but his faith was unshakeable – he was a true Christian. On the day he died, having been ill for weeks, I went down from Penarth to see him. Leaving, I said my goodbye about 8 p.m. When I got home I rang the farm but he had already passed away. I often wonder if he hung on until I got there? It helps me to think that I meant so much to him.

He and Aunty Lisa were childless, and had fostered one of my father's sisters, Annie, when she was 7 years old, training her to become their maid when she left school. This, of course, was another case of injustice to a child! I called her Aunty Annie, a true aunt, being my father's sister. She was five feet tall. Poor Aunt Annie had to work hard for very little pay. The elder couple would justify this by saying to her, "Don't forget we are feeding and clothing you". I discovered in later years that she had polycystic ovary syndrome, which meant that she could never have children. Looking back I believe that I was taken into the household by the elderly couple in order to fill a gap in Aunt Annie's life, so that she could bring me up as her own.

In my early days on the farm, the older folk enjoyed teasing me, and as a child I must have been a source of entertainment to them. In those times, a rabbit catcher used to come once a year with gin traps to catch the furry friends. The mole catchers also came with the skin being sent away to make clothes. The mole catcher was Clifford Jones. Cliff liked to tease visiting ministers to his chapel by telling the Reverend that they both did the same work. When asked what that work was he would say, "I bring them from darkness to the light!"

Looking back I find it difficult to believe that I, a child, was made to sleep in the same bed as the farm servant who was much older. There were many servants over the years and I was made to share a bed with each one of them. I remember the farm servants well – it was a happy relationship with all six who, in chronological order were, Lewis Harries, Emrys Rees, Elwyn Elias, a cousin, Hywel Morris, Tom Griffiths and Ronnie Cannell. All stayed for some two years each.

I was truly fortunate that I was not abused or bullied in any way. On the contrary, until I was ten or eleven, they were more like uncles, caring for me, and when I was older they were more like brothers. The change of farm servants occurred at

Michaelmas. No papers were signed – just a handshake. We had no problems getting workers, my aunties made excellent food and so the word got around that she kept 'an excellent table'.

The most loveable and dear of all the farm servants was Tom. Tom would come home late having been up to the village square in Croeslan where eight or ten other farm servants would congregate to chat and do mischief. If a young lady went by, they would scratch the pavement with their boots – similar to when a stallion meets his mare! The local chapel minister lived 50 yards down the road and would often receive a phone call from the lads, from a telephone box on the square. When he answered the phone, all he would hear was "Rrrrwp" – a farting noise! Nothing was said. It was all innocent fun, and there was never any vandalism, fighting or serious disorder. How life has changed.

Tom's two-year stay was so happy. His stories were legendary. The one we both enjoyed most was of his time at Capel Cynon Primary School. The headmaster, Mr Jones, lived with his wife in the school house next to the school, and every Monday, she would hang the washing on the line. Tom and his friends, Marteine Arfryn especially, would throw stones at the clothing, aiming mostly at Mrs Jones's underwear. The only way they could be sure the stone had struck the correct article was to put some mud on the stone, which would then leave a mark. Tom struck the target with uncanny accuracy!

Tom bought an old motor cycle, a Triumph. It had no starter and had to be pushed to a good speed before engaging gear. Tom and I would often spend Saturday afternoons repairing the machine. In the evening, he would take me on the pillion to the picture house in Rhydlewis hall. On the way back we had to climb a steep hill and halfway up, things would come to a stop. My job then was to dismount, push Tom and the motorcycle to the top and jump on again when on the flat.

He spoke much about girls, and one would believe he was

an expert on the courting business, but I am sure he did not court a girl in his life. He remained a bachelor.

I don't know if I was supposed to work on the farm as a servant when Uncle Evan retired, but when they saw me being accepted to go to medical school, the farm was sold the same year, when all three moved to a small holding nearby. This was eventually too much for Aunty Annie when the older couple died, and she moved to my cottage in the nearby village of Croeslan. She was then 70 years old, and stayed there for fourteen years, which, on looking back, I am pleased to have been able to do for her. Becoming less active and suffering from various disabilities, she was fortunate to have friends who cared for her and members of the family were also frequent callers. The old Welsh proverb is true – 'Better a near friend than a distant relative'.

It is the harvests that I remember mostly. People would come from a wide area to help with the haymaking, picking potatoes, etc. The farmers took their turn at haymaking, with no arguments as to whose turn it was next. My aunts used to make ginger beer, with bottles popping in the heat. They had a high alcohol content and after a long day in the sunshine the journey home was longer for some, going from side to side, hedge to hedge.

Despite the good times, I have no doubt whatsoever that being fostered damaged me emotionally. I know six people who went through a similar ordeal, and they all suffered lifelong mental damage. Two were Sisters in hospitals that I worked in. One attempted suicide, but survived. She came to lunch after I mentioned I was writing this book. Her poignant comment was that she had suffered from a failure to form relationships. She had been married twice, divorced each time and could not love another person. Two others had attempted suicide at some point in their lives, and all six had been admitted for a period to psychiatric hospitals for therapy.

I do not blame my parents. They thought that fostering was

best for me in the circumstances. It was common in Wales and large families eased their financial burden by fostering their children with other families where there were no children. However, I am convinced that the best place for a child is with his own family.

I am grateful to the Alltycnydau family for fostering me. I have no doubt that Uncle Evan and Aunty Lisa had great pleasure seeing my successes at school and college, and later as a doctor. They in turn had a little farm servant who worked hard for nothing for years and Aunt Annie had the joy of bringing up a 'son'. There is an old Welsh proverb, which is very appropriate, that I put on Aunt Annie's gravestone: "Eil fam, modryb dda" (A good aunt is a second mother).

PRIMARY AND GRAMMAR SCHOOLS

I ATTENDED COEDYBRYN PRIMARY School and soon ran into difficulties because of the nature of the school. Children who failed their 11+ entrance exams to the grammar school at Llandysul remained at the primary school until they were 15 years old. Secondary modern education did not as yet exist. Unfortunately, this meant that the younger children were forced to play and mix with older and rougher children, which meant that many of the young children often suffered mentally and physically from bullying and rough treatment. Nevertheless, I made many friends there, one was Ricey Thomas, who went on to be HMI for schools.

The farm was two miles from school, and I had to walk the two miles back and forth each day. This was very difficult for a young child as the road to school had very steep hills in both directions. It was often dark before I started the morning journey, and I found this unpleasant. Walking on the dark, lonely country road was not the best thing for a frightened child whose mind conjured all kinds of possible horrors on the route. Occasionally in the summer there would be a horse-drawn gypsy caravan, tucked into the hedge by the side of the road. The horse would be grazing, tied to a post nearby, with a greyhound tethered to one of the wheels.

On dark winter days, I was glad to reach a half way mark where my friends Gerald and Cecil lived. I would be welcomed by Tom and Rachel Davies, Nursery, and their children Doreen, Nancy and Ifor. I would walk into the house without knocking as if it were my own home, such was the warmth of their kindness and welcome.

Gerald and Cecil would accompany me on the rest of my journey up the long steep hill to school. Amid the happy memories are unpleasant ones – especially of bullying suffered and witnessed. I can remember a pleasant 13-year-old boy from Estonia who came to the school. He was staying locally and his parents were probably refugees during the war. Because he was a foreigner he was equated in the minds of the children with the German enemy and they took it out on him. Some of the older boys decided to give him a beating on the way home. I was a small boy then and I can remember vividly seeing him being punched and badly beaten.

As a doctor, I saw much physical abuse during my working life. When I was working with children, babies used to come in with fractures and bruises, a fall downstairs always the cause. Some died, and the coroner in the inquest would agree – accidental. By now, doctors, paediatricians and pathologists are more alert to the situation, and give the correct diagnosis and punishment for those responsible.

Very often the bullying would take place behind the facade of respectability with the victim afraid to speak out. There was a case in my practice of a wife always being bruised around the head and elsewhere, a fall being blamed. I have no doubt, with hindsight, that the injuries were the result of domestic violence. The husband seemed to be the nicest of people, but he was probably a case of what we call in Welsh 'angel pen ffordd a diawl pen tân' (an angel in public but a devil in his own home). A doctor working as a GP often wonders what different kinds of mental and physical cruelty goes on behind respectable doors.

I did well at school and showed such promise that the headmistress insisted I sit the 11+ when I was a little over 10 years old rather than a year later as I should have. She assured my aunt and uncle that I was certain to succeed. Her prophecy was correct, but I have no doubt now, looking back on my life, that it was a big mistake to go to the grammar school in Llandysul so young. It is so important that a child has time to mature in all ways, socially and emotionally. When I read of children who have been coached by their parents and forced into studies and activities, which other children do not do until a later age, I feel very sorry for them. I have no doubt that the child prodigy in study or sport is a very immature and unhappy person.

However, my time at Llandysul Grammar School was, perhaps, the happiest of my life. It was a grammar school in a country area, with only 450 pupils, and discipline was lax. Most of the teachers were excellent. The headmaster was a portly Latin scholar, and a graduate of Jesus College, Oxford – T Edgar Davies. He was very short, only just over five feet, which earned him the nickname 'Davies Bach'. He was always immaculately dressed with a gold chain and gold coin hanging over his waistcoat. His hobby was his Pekinese dog, which always greeted him as he took his ritual walk to his residence on the school grounds during the dinner hour. His favourite saying was, "Common sense, the rarest of all senses". I found later in life how true that was. He lived a life totally isolated from the community and after retiring he returned to his native Newport, Monmouthshire.

My first term started well when I won the Evan Morgan Scholarship for being one of the top four in the whole of Cardiganshire entering grammar schools in 1944 – a cheque for £7.50. I never saw any of the prize money. I gave the cheque to my aunt and heard no more of it!

For growing boys in their teens, the arrival of young, new female teachers was an event. Three new teachers, all female, arrived at this time. One of them wore a skirt shorter than the other two, and sat in front of the class with legs a little apart! Four of the boys sat directly in front of her, four rows back. They found much interest in the young lady, and we heard a few pencils falling to the floor that had to be recovered by bending down! "What colour today?" asked one of the lads.

"Not sure", said the one that had bent down.

"Have another look, then", and down went another pencil. The teacher had no idea what was going on!

We had lunch in school, although the locals from the village often went home. This was the time to enjoy an excellent two-course meal, followed by games. My favourite pudding was, and still is, spotted dick, drowned in custard. One or two of the senior lads would sell theirs for sixpence, and eventually I found out why – to buy cigarettes. The most famous was Cyril Thomas, an international fly-fisherman. Eventually his heavy smoking took its toll, and he died of lung disease at the age of fifty. On his tombstone in the local churchyard are the words, 'Gone Fishing'.

I must mention one of the teachers, Mr Sweet. He was over six feet tall, with a bad limp, having lost part of his leg during the war. His experiences in the trenches in France had affected his nerves, and he was erratic in his responses. Teachers in those days were allowed to clout pupils on the ears. My late uncle, the famous Welsh poet and novelist, T Llew Jones, told me of the day Mr Sweet was marking one of his English essays, which was of an extremely high standard. Mr Sweet did not believe that he could write so well and that the work was his own, and he was called to the front of the class. "Did you write this?" asked Mr Sweet. "Yes, Sir", replied T Llew Jones and he was immediately given a clout on his ear!

Children can be cruel and one or two would torment the teachers. Mr Sweet's nerves were bad and he suffered from what was then called 'shell shock'. This did not prevent the children from tormenting him. On the 5th of November 1947, Guy Fawkes Day, Mr Sweet happened to be out in the school yard invigilating at break time. One of the senior boys had a huge firework and placed it behind him, lit it and ran. There was a massive bang and Mr Sweet, poor man, jumped a foot into the air!

I found Mr Sweet to have a nature as good as his name. Following the 1947 snowfall, the most on record in the area, few pupils got to school. No bus could travel, so I cycled. Mr Sweet was taking the religious instruction lesson that day, and we had to read a verse each. I couldn't cope with reading in class, and, unknown to him, one of my friends would read for me. My friend was away, so I had to tell Mr Sweet the truth. I can still remember his kind words to me regarding my stammer, "Never mind, my boy, a lot of people have had the same affliction, including the present King George VI and it hasn't restricted their success in life." Kind words have an effect for good that we cannot measure.

Woodwork was one of my favourite subjects. In the third year, the homework was drawing a bit that fitted into a brace to manually drill a hole in wood. One of my friends got 95 per cent, but when my turn came I got 98 per cent. I must be honest, it could have been favouritism, for the teacher, Santley Jones, came from Beulah and was a great friend of my Uncle Dewi!

The hard manual work on the farm meant I was a very strong young man. This contributed to my winning the Champion Junior Boy in the school sports day of 1948, under fifteen years of age, for my house 'Tysul'. Being a poor runner, my specialities were throwing: discus, weight, javelin and cricket ball – and I came first in all four. This led to me representing the school in discus throwing in the Inter County Sports in Carmarthen. Cardiganshire and Carmarthenshire were together then. I won again, this time breaking the county record, despite never having been taught how to throw – sheer strength and little technique. The All Wales competition came next, in Wrexham. I was very disappointed to come fourth, especially as the winner threw less than I had in Carmarthen. Control of 'nerves' would have helped!

My O level results were good, and in the September, I went back to the sixth form at fourteen to do A level physics, chemistry and biology. Tim, the physics master, was excellent. So was Llew Chem, but the biology master read the syllabus to us on the first day, and we had to get on with it – essays every week and only one formal lesson in two years, and that was when the HMI was in the class! I realised something had to be done, and on my own initiative, I wrote to Foyles, the bookshop in London, to get *Lowson's Botany* and Grove and Newell's *Animal Biology* – the best in the field.

To make up for the lack of instruction in biology I made

an effort to teach myself everything. Dissection was important and I taught myself, catching animals on the farm – rabbits, etc. – and dissecting them in the garage. I can honestly say that having to do this on my own probably gave me a more thorough knowledge of the subject than if I had been taught in class by a teacher – 'practice is better than a teacher', after all. Looking back I can see now that my surgical ability was in no little part due to this early enforced dissection in the farm garage!

When A levels came, I had 3 As at sixteen. Unfortunately, I was too young to enter university so there was no choice but to go back to school. There was no such thing as a gap year in those days. To entice me to stay on at school the headmaster made me head prefect.

During the extra year at school, I had several interviews to enter medical schools – Charing Cross and Cardiff, the Welsh National School of Medicine. Charing Cross would take me with open arms, but I had to wait until I was eighteen and that would have meant wasting another year! One of those on the committee in London asked had I played cricket against Tregaron Grammar School, the headmaster having put on my reference that I played cricket for the school. I later learned he was Dr William Evans, a famous heart specialist, of Tyndomen Farm near Tregaron! The reasoning for the age eighteen was what they considered to be my lack of maturity: they felt students had to be eighteen to cope with medical studies.

However, after a month of disappointment, a letter arrived to say that Cardiff was ready to take me, starting October 1951. I felt on top of the world, and my pranks in school increased, despite my being head prefect.

The headmaster had a bell by his office door which controlled the school timing. He rang it every day without fail, and it was the focal point that kept the school running smoothly and on time. I had discovered that the batteries, actually old Leclanche cells, were hidden in the chemistry laboratory upstairs, connected in parallel, so that two wires touching would activate the whole bell system. I decided to play a prank on the headmaster. When the headmaster would be coming from his house to his room at 1.40 p.m. after lunching at home, I would activate the bell from upstairs, without anybody touching the button. The headmaster's movements were visible from the chemistry laboratory, and with a crowd of my friends hanging around, but nobody near his door, he arrived. My timing was perfect, I touched the wires, off went the bell and he stood paralysed, staring at a bell five yards away that was ringing of its own accord. He was heard to say, "There must be a ghost here!"

I'm afraid I filled my plentiful spare time by playing other pranks. Once again the aim was to cause disruption and bamboozle the headmaster who was a time and motion man and did everything at the appointed time. The target this time was the school clock according to which the headmaster personally rang the bell every day. The head prefect was the only pupil allowed to have a copy of the master key to the whole school. This opened the door to the clock tower, which was always locked. It was important that I went home early one day, and so I decided with my friend Odwyn to enter the tower and manipulate the clock hands, putting them forward fifteen minutes. The headmaster naturally rang the bell as usual according to the clock and the whole school was dismissed early!

Discovering from his teaching staff that the bell had been fifteen minutes early, the headmaster launched an investigation, and the conclusion was that there was a mechanical problem in the workings of the clock itself! It was Friday afternoon, and the caretaker had to spend the weekend checking every nut and bolt, oiling everything that could have been responsible.

Until I entered the sixth form my hair had been cut somewhat crudely by friends, Evan and Benji Evans, the sons of the neighbouring farm, Tower Hill. In the sixth form, I decided that I should become more sophisticated and suave and have my hair cut properly. My co-pupils went to a barber's shop in Llandysul on the main street. It was considered by adolescent males to be the place to go to for more than one reason.

After having my hair done I decided to do what my friends told me to do and ask for what were considered to be 'goods' that should not be talked about. The barber said, "How many packets do you want?" To be truthful, I had no idea what he meant, but with others present, replied, "One".

Having paid and departed, I became inquisitive and, out of sight, opened the container. Inside were three condoms! I replaced them in my pocket and went home. Walking down the lane to the farm, I thought, what if my aunties see them? Some 100 yards from the house, I dug a hole in the hedge, some 5 feet from the ground, and deposited them there, and that's where, to my knowledge, they still are!

My best friend at school was a brilliant boy, Trefor Owen. He was killed flying his jet plane when he crashed at Trevose Head on the north Cornish coast on the 7th of July 1955. He was a boy always up to all kinds of adventurous and daring experiments. I remember one time when he put a live bullet in a vice in his father's workshop, opened the window, hammered a nail into the live part and BANG out flew the bullet through the window into the sky! He experimented with making his own fireworks from sulphur, saltpetre and charcoal, and burnt two fingers badly.

He was two years older than me, and I sat next to him for three years. He could have succeeded in any subject, but decided in the first year of the sixth form to go to Cranwell College, where he qualified as flight lieutenant. The RAF moved him to Cornwall. He was given his own jet plane, and would fly back to Wales, doing all kinds of tricks with his aeroplane over the old school in Llandysul to the great delight of the pupils and the annoyance of the headmaster.

His father asked me to accompany him to his funeral in Bwlchygroes. I came home from medical school especially. It was a harrowing day and his death was a great blow to me.

THE MEDICAL STUDENT

THERE WERE A FEW things that influenced my decision to choose medicine as a career. A severe stammer prevented me from teaching or lecturing or preaching! Observing people, with their differences, physical and psychological gave me much interest and pleasure. My friend Ifor Davies had started in Cardiff Medical School and the whole neighbourhood was very impressed with this. He used to study in a peaceful location – in a disused chicken shed in a field overlooking the village. I felt that if he could succeed, so could I.

I felt that all my dissection in the garage on the farm had taught me a lot and would be helpful for surgery. However, none of my family on either side had been doctors – they had been farmers, craftsmen, preachers or teachers!

When I was in the sixth form, without my knowing, Aunty Lisa and Uncle Evan had been to see the headmaster, Edgar Davies, to ask him had I enough ability to succeed. A basketful of fresh eggs from the farm was the gift for his time, how could he say no?

Before departing from the country to the big city, I was given lots of advice from various people. One was Ben Howell Jones, a local carpenter, who had been in the navy. His words were, "Beware of the homosexuals, there are many of them in Cardiff!" Truthfully, my knowledge of this aspect of sex was nil, although I had read articles in the papers about such things. The best way to recognise them, said BHJ, was the fact that they wore suede shoes! For the first three months my eyes always looked down when walking on the city pavements! On my first meeting with my father-in-law, what was he wearing? Suede shoes! Was my friend serious in his advice, or was he pulling my leg?

Ben was a character, very typical of those bred in rural areas, and he had a story for every occasion. Employed by

Cardiganshire County Council at its office in Lampeter, he met a lady who took his fancy, which led to courting. This took place on winter nights in the office, and eventually the boss found out. He was called before the boss and accused of using electricity for lighting and heating, paid for of course by the local people as rates, after offices closed at 5 p.m. "That's not true," answered Ben, "we were courting in the dark!" They were later married – to each other!

The most important procedure of the first day in college was registration, over sixty of us. The registrar called out my name "Joshua Gerwyn Elias". Most of the students were English speaking, and I was immediately christened "Josh"; to this day the medical profession recognise me as Josh.

An invitation arrived to go to the freshers' dance on the Saturday night. I was a country lad, brought up on a farm, and knew nothing at all about dancing. I remember going to the dancing school under the Continental restaurant in Queen Street. Starting with the easiest, the waltz, the kind lady kept repeating one, two, three, but to a lad with two left feet, it took a very long time. She went home many a night with feet bruised up to her ankles!

Anatomy and physiology were the first subjects I studied, the former necessitating dissecting the human body. I had never seen a dead person, and in the room there were fifteen corpses. Facing this was not easy, but it had to be done and I decided to go on my own the first time. The bodies were stark and naked laid out on trestles or tables. They had been preserved with formalin and soaked in it for weeks or months. The smell of formalin was nauseating! The corpses were in rows, on their backs, with the upper half at an angle of 45°, so that it would be easier to dissect the upper part of the body and the head and neck. On the right there were sinks, and plenty of hot and cold water with soap to wash afterwards. No gloves were used. We were told in no uncertain terms to respect the deceased. Four students left the course in the first week because they found the work repulsive.

Among the demonstrators was a famous surgeon, Mr J O D Wade. He was operating one morning when, leaning forward, his tummy touched the operating table and he felt a pain. When he was examined later by one of his friends, cancer of the stomach was diagnosed. He decided to spend his remaining months teaching students the art of dissection. His five sons became doctors. He was a wonderful man.

When the second MB examinations came after eighteen months, the written papers went well. Next were vivas, where one came face to face with the examiner and had to answer his questions. I remember the anatomy exam when the professor exposed the upper leg in a dissected body. "What's this muscle?"

I replied, *"Gluteus medius,* the one little dogs use to pee against a tree". He frowned at me and told me not to waste his time, and asked me whether I wanted to be a doctor or vet! He then pointed to a part of the brain and asked, "What's this?"

"Substantia Nigra," I replied, "degeneration of which causes Parkinson's Disease." More questions followed, which I knew the answer to. As I left I said, "Thank you, Sir", hoping it would give me an extra mark! I passed.

Afterwards, there were celebrations, but I must be honest, I was too tired to indulge. All I needed was sleep, and that for a week.

In front of me was a big signpost, one arm of which pointed to the Cardiff Royal Infirmary, the centre for the clinical part of the course. It was a privilege to go there and to do what I wanted most – be a doctor who could make a difference for good by learning all about human beings and their illnesses.

The first lecture was by the professor of medicine, Harold Scarborough, a highly respected man in the medical world. He was over six feet tall, and the collar of his white coat always stuck up towards his ear. Everybody expected big stuff, and we got it. He entered the theatre like a ballet dancer, looked around, said nothing as he wrote on the board, "What am I doing here?" No notes.

His first words were that every lecturer should excite, spur and entertain. He did all three. Reiterating the sentence with emphasis on the four important words, 'What', 'I', 'doing' and 'here', an hour went by. One of his comments was that nobody could remember all the answers to the problems in medicine, but it was important to know where to find them. After qualifying, I had the pleasure of being his house physician for six months, picking up all the gems that came from his mouth.

One morning at 7 a.m., doing his house job, a woman of eighty was admitted from the Canton area. She was barely conscious, and her temperature was 84°F instead of 97°. After I had performed all the tests the professor arrived on the scene. He asked me why I was up so early and what tests had I done, but then he said I should have done the serum magnesium. The consultants always wanted to show they knew more than their juniors! The diagnosis of course was hypothermia. The professor's comments on magnesium were correct, in that all hibernating animals, such as the hedgehog, have a very high level of magnesium after sleeping for months.

In our transitional term, we were split into groups of six, with different consultants. I happened to be with Professor Scarborough but never saw him, because his deputies were entrusted with teaching us the basics. One day, nobody was concentrating on his teaching and he said, "Are you listening to me or watching the pretty nurses?" The truth was we were doing both, always!

Our first lecture by the professor of surgery, Lambert Rogers, was on head injuries, with special attention to motorcycle injuries. His words have always stayed with me, that 30 per cent of deaths in men between eighteen and thirty were due to going too fast on two wheels. His way of decreasing the pressure on the brain after injury was to use Epsom salts enemas, which are out of fashion by now. I remember one of my patients who had a head injury asking me when he regained consciousness, whether I had understood his problems, because his injury was to the head and not his bottom!

It was during this term that a letter arrived from the department of obstetrics (midwifery), saying that they were going to start doing artificial insemination by donor. I had seen this in animals in my native area, known as 'Tarw Potel'. This was for those couples that could not have children due to the husband being sterile, usually due to mumps. Semen was needed, and the suggestion was that medical students would give a good supply! The fee was £5 a time, which was good considering my grant, which was used to cover everything – digs, food, etc. – was £60 a term. A physical examination had to be performed. The colour of the hair and eyes were important to match the husband. I gave it thought, and answered "No", because it would worry me thinking that a child of mine, whom I didn't know, could be getting a dreadful upbringing and be abused.

Years afterwards, in the practice, a couple with three sons came on to my list. Visiting the house one day because one of the sons was ill, seeing the photos on the wall, I mentioned how much like their father the children all were. The mother came to the surgery a few days later and said that her husband was not the children's father; he was sterile, and with his permission, whenever they wanted a child, she would spend the weekend with her GP! Had the General Medical Council found out, he would have been struck off.

Pharmacology, knowing all about medicines, good and bad, was next on the list of subjects. The lecturer reminded me of a GP in Henllan, who was quite a character. A call came from a farm, two miles from the surgery, and off he went. Mrs Jones was ill and the 10-year-old son was asked to fetch her medicine, and to come to the surgery by 6 p.m. GPs mixed their own medicine in those days. The boy arrived, medicine not ready, so he was asked into the dispensary. The doctor put a spoonful of red crystals in the bottle, filled it with water from the tap, cork on and shook. As he was mixing, the GP was told by the boy that he knew what was wrong with his mother. "Thirst", said the boy. "You've filled the medicine bottle with water!"

Once, a farmer went to the surgery complaining of insomnia. There were no sleeping tablets in those days, and the doctor said, "Drink half a bottle of whisky."

"What if it doesn't work?" said the farmer.

"Oh" said the doctor, "Drink the other half". The doctor loved his drink, and one day in Newcastle Emlyn, he met one of his friends, a famous local auctioneer, and agreed to go for a pint. They left their cars outside, with the keys still inside, as was the habit in those days. Both cars were the same colour and make. Having had his fill, the doctor had to leave, and jumped into the car. The petrol gauge showed low, so he filled up in the garage. As he went home, he saw an old friend by the roadside and stopped to chat. "A new car?" asked the friend. It was only then that he noticed he was driving the auctioneer's car!

The main corridor of the hospital was about 100 yards long, and at one end, by the front door, was a famous painting hanging from the wall, 9 feet tall and 6 feet wide, of a war time scene in the Mametz Ward of the hospital. The characters were the matron, Montgomery Wilson and surgeon, commanding officer, Lieutenant Colonel Hepburn with the injured soldiers. In December 1953, with Christmas approaching, and the students in a festive mood, one of them had a bet with his friends that he would ride a bicycle naked at midnight from one end of the corridor to the other. I don't know if he had been drinking, but, with dozens watching, male and female, off he went at a good speed, in case the night sister caught him. However, he was going too fast and failed to stop at the end of the corridor and the wheel of his bike went straight through the painting. When I arrived at the CRI the next morning, it was obvious there was a problem, because the place was silent like a mortuary. Investigations followed. He was called in front of the hospital committee and had to pay a large sum for repairs, the painting being removed for renovation. I doubt if what he obtained from the bet was sufficient to pay the expenses.

It wasn't only the students that were naughty. The nurses' home was adjoining the hospital and the night sister had to lock the door at 10.30 p.m. to keep the nurses in, and the male students out! One night, I was working in casualty, and had gone to bed about 1 a.m., all being quiet. There was a mighty knock on my door before I'd managed to fall asleep. It was the porter, who said, "Come quickly". I put my trousers on, my white coat, no socks, and off I went. Sister led me to a tree outside the nurses' home, with a nurse half way up, crying and in severe pain. We learnt later that she had been leaving a window open near the tree, which she climbed when she came in after the front door was locked. It was a wet night and she had slipped on the tree, and one of the branches penetrated her front passage and out through her tummy.

I gave her a morphia injection that eased the pain a little. The branch was sawn and she was brought down. The anaesthetist was there by then, at the bottom of the trunk, and put her to sleep, out of her pain. The theatre was ready and I operated on her, opening the abdomen and removing the wood carefully. After making sure the bleeding had stopped, I closed the incision and stitched her up. She went home in a few days.

I didn't see her again for three years, but one day when I was working at the midwifery department over the road from the hospital, who came in with a big fat belly but her, obviously pregnant having married a year before. She gave me a big hug. She was in labour, her first child, and off we went to the delivery room where a lovely baby boy was born with the use of a Wrigley's forceps. She named him Joshua! When she left the hospital tears of joy flowed down her cheeks. I think I also cried – words were not necessary. For a doctor there is no such joy as the joy of success.

I went back to stay with my uncle and aunt for my summer holiday in 1953. They had retired from the farm and moved to a house in the village. My first holiday lasted three months, but the future ones were confined to only one month, as we had to spend time with the patients and their illnesses. My uncle had a Ford Prefect, EBX 762, which I was allowed to drive. Two of my friends, Ricey and Iori, were with me one day, driving through the village. On a slight bend I was going too fast, and they swore that the car was on two wheels!

One day during that holiday, I played for the Old Boys' cricket team against the school in Llandysul. One of my friends from the village, Gareth Thomas, was bowling for the pupils. He was a very fast bowler, and his first ball flattened my wicket. I was not asked to play for the Old Boys again!

Gareth was very kind to me on the 3rd of March 1998, the day, unbelievably, both my mother and my aunt died. Yes, the very same day! My siblings organised my mother's funeral in Capel-y-Wig near Llangrannog, where my father was buried. Aunty Annie had told me a month before that she wished to be buried near her friends, Gwilym and Evan Jones of Glyniscoed, their stepmother being Uncle Evan's sister. "There is no need to go down to Narberth", were her words. That is, no cremation. No plot had been arranged, and there wasn't an obvious one. Looking through the rows, there was only one unused near where she preferred, one that had been booked by Gareth for himself. Eventually, I got him on the phone, at his carpet-selling business in the market place in Carmarthen and he said that he did not need his arranged resting place –we could use it. What a relief. My aunt is buried there, near her friends. Another lesson – get arrangements right years before the inevitable day. A degree in the university of life is harder than one in medicine!

CLINICAL STUDIES

THE TIME CAME TO return to Cardiff. It was a Sunday afternoon, and I had been to chapel in the morning. After the usual excellent lunch, off I went to catch the bus on the square at Croeslan and then the train from Carmarthen. "Be good", was the advice from my aunties, and I gave them a kiss each and shook my uncle's hand. On the platform, the smoke and steam from the train's engine could be seen from a distance. There were many students there, waiting, with different scarves from various colleges in south Wales and beyond.

A bus ride towards St Fagans took me to my lodgings in Llandaff, where my landlady gave me a warm welcome, having been lonely for the three months without her lodger. A cup of tea was refreshing, followed by preparation for my first day on the wards as a real medical student.

When Monday morning arrived I went to the hospital with a clean shirt, white coat, stethoscope, patella hammer to elicit the tendon reflexes, a hat pin to test skin sensation and a little book to record facts about patients. I at least looked like a doctor! There was much commotion with everyone looking at the notice boards to see where we were to go, which hospital, which consultant, medicine or surgery. It was exciting! In the next three years we would be meeting almost every consultant in Cardiff.

The first, Dr D A Williams, known as 'D A', a consultant physician in Llandough Hospital, who specialized in asthma, which he had suffered from since a child. He was very kind to my Aunt Lisi, of Cwrrws Farm, near Henllan, who was also an asthma sufferer. During her most severe attacks of asthma, I would bring her to Cardiff to see D A. This happened six times, and D A succeeded in making her better on each occasion. Indeed, I can remember her in a bad way gasping for her 'last' breath as she went through the hospital door, but seeing D A Williams was sufficient! Faith often works miracles in the world of medicine. The truths that D A told us as students are still imprinted on my mind. One of his favourite sayings was, "There are two ways to be a good doctor. Know your stuff and be kind to patients". He did both. Another of his sayings was, "It's nice to be important but more important to be nice".

However, there were days when he could be strict, and he could get very angry when faced with incompetence. A lady came in one day, and died very soon after. D A felt that the GP had been too slow in sending her into hospital. His comment was, "An architect covers his mistakes with ivy, an artist with paint, and a doctor with earth!"

D A was always thorough in his work. He taught us first how to take a good history of the patient's present complaint, with name, age and address on top of the page. This was followed by the date of onset, and what was felt or seen. Were there headaches, a cough, tummy ache, water problems, joint pains, etc.? His questions were relevant to what he thought was the correct diagnosis. The history of the patient came next – had there been similar symptoms before? Family history was important because of genetic abnormalities.

Lastly, he looked at the patient's social life. How much alcohol was consumed? Did he or she smoke? What were their hobbies? Did they find mixing with others easy? Next came the examination, starting with the external features, skin and eyes. Was there jaundice, for example? What condition was the hair? Was there swelling in the legs or lymph glands? And then he examined the heart, blood pressure, lungs, abdomen and urinary system, ending with the central nervous system.

By now, the doctor should have some idea of what was wrong. Tests followed to confirm the diagnosis. The above has been the basis of a doctor's work, old or young, for centuries. Experience tells us that 90 per cent of medical opinions are made on the history alone. For example, a man on the ward had a dreadful cough, bringing up purulent sputum, and one day, he brought up a cupful at once. D A told us there could be only one cause – a lung abscess. "Listen to the patient. He is telling you what is wrong with him."

The next week, after his ward round, D A talked about careful observation. He started by saying that one did not have to be clever to be a good doctor. What was important was good observation and memory to see a disease and remember it, then recognise when it next turned up. He used the mouth and tongue as examples, and how changes helped to discover the exact nature of the illness. Tragically, there has been a big increase in disease of the mouth in the last few years. Cancer of this area is thirty times more common in those that smoke and drink alcohol.

One day, D A spent a long time with a patient suffering from diabetes mellitus, excess sugar in the body, blood, urine, etc. He told us about the doctors of bygone days, before modern tests, having to taste the urine. Another method, especially in men, was to get six or seven together, one with the suspected condition, and ask them to wee by a hedge. The one with the most flies on his boots had it. Why? There was sugar in his urine, some landed on his footwear, and the flying friends knew where it was, like a sugar pot on the table at teatime.

The subject that I was interested in was surgery, and I spent the next three months with Mr Ioan-Jones, senior consultant surgeon at the CRI. He was excellent with breast operations, especially cancer. Nine out of every hundred women suffer from it at some point in their lives, but modern treatment has improved the outlook out of all recognition. In his time, removal, either the lumps or the whole breast was standard but now, drugs, before or after surgery, have changed the prognosis, with life expectancy in decades. I have seen two men with the disease.

Why these hyphenated names? Many of them are Jones, Davies or Williams, etc. I remember one with three names, and the explanation given was that they were not sure who his father was!

Mr Ioan-Jones's registrar was Mr L P Thomas, known as 'L P', as good a surgeon as the chief himself. After becoming consultant surgeon in Newport, I asked him to operate on a good friend of mine from Ffostrasol. This was done successfully in St Winifred's Hospital in Cardiff. Every year since, on his way to New Quay for his summer holidays, he would call to see how she was getting on, and was always rewarded with a basketful of eggs in his car boot!

All the surgeons had to do a day attending to emergency admissions. One day, a woman of fifty came in with intestinal obstruction, blockage in the bowels. Ioan-Jones was not to be seen, so L P did the job, successfully. Two days later, she was still on a drip as no food was allowed for some time. Ioan did a ward round, teaching students. With a narrow Roman nose, he sniffed quite often, and approached this person's bed. The sign to watch for to make sure that all had gone well was if the patient was passing wind: there was nothing else to pass because no food had been eaten by the patient. Ioan-Jones asked, after a sniff, "Have you passed wind?" "No", said the patient, "I think it was the woman in the next bed".

Summer followed, and back to Llandough, with another physician, Dr Byron Evans. Born in Llanon, he still had the fresh air from Cardigan Bay in his nostrils. Educated in London, some of the time with Sir Horace Evans, later Lord Evans of Merthyr Tydfil, sometime physician to the Queen. I am not being disrespectful to the noble lord, but Dr William Sargent's words about honours awarded to doctors are interesting. He was, by the way, head of the Maudsley Hospital in London, the famous psychiatric institution. Dr Sargent said, "I learnt very early on, that you don't progress in the medical world by being a good doctor, but for political and social reasons. It was late in life that Fleming, discoverer of penicillin, was knighted. Florey, an administrator, was made 'Lord'. It is helping patients that brings the greatest happiness in life, not playing politics, not sitting on forty or more committees hoping to receive accolades." So true.

Back to Byron. He was very different from D A. An exhibitionist at times but an excellent diagnostician, although he failed to diagnose my father who died at fifty-four of primary amyloidosis. He had great pleasure going back to Cardiganshire for his holidays. The local GPs seemed to know when he was about and often asked him to see a patient, sometimes a farmer in an isolated location, who had been in bed ill for weeks. He would give his opinion on the spot and then take him into Llandough to prove he was right. A big demonstration to the students followed if correct, as was usually the case. With much 'Hwyl', the jokes would fly. He was a great comforter to the weak, and an excellent teacher to the young students, especially if you were Welsh. We shared an affliction, a stammer, which brought us together, and imitations of his speech, "B-B-B-Byron" annoyed me. Strangely, when we spoke to each other, neither of us stammered.

He brought London etiquette to Llandough. The ward round would be like a snake: he, sister and his registrar in front, the latter having had to wait for him by the front door of the hospital, with discussion of events and problems on the way in. Along to Ward E1, where sister, house physician, students and physiotherapists would be congregated together, quiet when he came around the corner. Greeted by sister, we would proceed to the patients' beds, all of whom were tidily tucked in, bedclothes immaculate, etc. He decided what tests were necessary, when the patient would go home, and so on.

Every student was allocated a patient, having to know all about him or her. A friend of mine was in the group, and Byron asked him to present 'the case'. After giving a good history, he said that the abdomen had a swelling on one side. He was made to recite the five causes of swollen tummy, all starting with the letter 'f', that is, fat, faeces, foetus, fluid and flatus. Byron bent over to examine the lump, could not find it, and said, "She must have passed it". There was much hilarity if the patient wasn't very ill.

Next, up to Ward E2, the men's ward where Sister Bronwen Jones, known affectionately as 'Bron' was waiting. Born in Aberdare, she spent her whole nursing life in Llandough Hospital until retiring at sixty to go home to nurse her elderly mother. 'Bron' lived to be over ninety, still a spinster. She was five feet tall, with no excess fat and had a good figure, but we never saw her face: it was always covered in thick layers of paint and powder. Her shoes were always spotless, and every hair was in its place. She nursed me when I was on her ward in 1968, and after being discharged, I composed some poems in appreciation of her care and sent them to her by post. Thirty years later, one of my friends, Mrs Scragg, who had also been her staff nurse, visited her home, and what did she bring out from her desk? The poems I had sent her so long ago.

Byron gave a party in his house to each group of students, jokes of course. One of his best was about the man with the glass eye. It was the practice then to take it out when retiring and insert in a cup of water by the bedside. Thirsty one night, after a few drinks, the man, half asleep, swallowed the water, eye and all. After three days, nothing had come through, so he went to see his GP who referred him to the local surgeon. This meant examination of the back passage and colon, that is, a sigmoidoscopy. Viewing through, the surgeon said "I see nothing amiss". "Strange", said the man, "I can see you".

During the fourth year we started studying pathology, and visits to the mortuary to see post mortems were essential. Many felt nervous the first time, including myself, but off we went after an introductory chat of five minutes by Professor Gough in the lecture theatre. Three students purposely took the wrong path, unable to stomach what was coming that day, maybe after a hard time the night before!

We entered the room; it was cold. A large room, about 30 metres long and 20 metres wide, with three trestles on the left, and on the right, eight steps, 15 metres long for us to observe proceedings, with no stools or chairs. The professor emphasised the importance of post mortems. If the cause of death was not known it could be murder, and a matter for the police.

One common reason for post mortems in south Wales was the effect of coal dust on colliers or coal-trimmers on ships loading in the docks in Cardiff. If the life of the dead person had been affected by dust, the widow would receive compensation, a pension and/or a lump sum.

On this morning, the professor used the body of a collier to show the changes that occur in the lungs from the effect of the coal dust, an easy subject that every student could see and understand. The body was wheeled into the room on a trolley, covered in a white sheet. It was placed on the trestle, and then the cover removed. Suddenly, with the room silent, a groan was heard and down went one of the female students – she had fainted. We took her out to the fresh air, where she recovered quickly, but did not return that day; in time she became accustomed to the experience. The technician, a policeman named Evans, who had retired from the force, opened the chest and tummy, and within five minutes, had every organ on the demonstration table in front of us – heart, lungs, stomach, bowels, kidneys and spleen. The brain came last. The professor showed the lungs and the pathological changes.

Writing about coal dust and its effect on the lungs, that is, pneumoconiosis, reminds me of a great character, Dai Evans, who lived in Penarth when I arrived in 1960. He was the youngest of five brothers, born and bred in one of the mining villages of Carmarthenshire, where the best coal, anthracite, was found, again proving my favourite saying, "Only the best from the west". With most of the locals, including Dai's father and four brothers already extracting the 'black gold' from the bowels of the earth, it was his turn to go down the pit when he left school at fourteen. But he was scared. An accident at a mine almost a year before had killed three people, and so he refused. What was he to do with no other reasonable employment in the area? Like many lads at the time, he ventured east, ending up in Penarth. When he got older, he married a local girl, Mary, and had seven children. By the time I saw him, his chest disease was advanced, he was short of breath and unable to venture outside the house overlooking the docks.

In the first half of the twentieth century, Penarth and Cardiff were famous for exporting coal, which came down from the valleys in train loads to the docks, the journey ending right next to the jetty where the empty ships would be waiting to load and sail all over the world. On the jetties were huge mechanical devices that, after loosening the truck from the train, would turn it towards the water and lift the back end, so that the coal would drop into the ship's hold. When full, it would start its journey out to sea when the tides allowed, through the sluice-gate and away with lofted sails. High tide occurs every twelve hours and twenty-five minutes and when low, there would be no water in the bay at all, hence the importance of the gates to keep the water in the dock and the ship afloat.

I asked one of my medical friends at the time, practising in a non-industrial area, why he thought Dai had developed the pneumoconiosis without being underground. My friend suggested that Mary had got fed up with having more and more children, that she relegated her husband to sleeping in the coalhouse at the back. Dragon as she was, she wasn't that cruel!

The real reason was he had become a coal-trimmer. It involved controlling the amount of coal that entered the hold of the ship, and where it went, not too much in the bow or stern in order not to unbalance the ship. During the movement of the load from truck to ship, large amounts of coal dust were produced and entered the atmosphere which was inhaled by the workers, mostly the coal-trimmers; hence the disease. After a long battle and much negotiating, the trimmers were compensated as were the miners for their condition.

TAPEWORMS AND A GOLD MEDAL

T HE FIFTH YEAR CAME, with no time for anything but work. I felt like a busy bee on a hot summer's day. Public health and forensic medicine were additional subjects with final examinations to pass in both. I gained practical experience in midwifery and lived in the maternity hospital for two months and was called upon to deliver at night if the need came. It is interesting to know that most babies are born at night. Why? Nobody knows!

Forensic medicine was interesting. The senior lecturer was Dr Lester James, who spent most of his summer holidays sailing in New Quay. His method of getting attention was to shock us, in words or photographs, usually at the beginning of a lecture. As chief pathologist to the South Wales Police, in addition to his lectureship and hospital work, the variety was endless. One day, before saying a word, he projected a slide on to the screen of a rugby player, six feet and four inches tall. This healthy strong young man had been 'friendly' with a married woman.

They were making love on the floor when the husband arrived home unexpectedly. He saw them and in his rage he immediately grabbed a kitchen knife and put it through the back of the lover's neck. The knife went through his spinal cord and he died on the spot. To prove what went on to the judge in court, Lester had taken a photograph of the man still lying face down, with the knife embedded in his neck. It was this slide that he showed us.

Interestingly, when the case came up in crown court, he was discharged without punishment because it was a crime of passion due to excessive provocation.

Another day, the lecture given was on births, marriages and deaths. By this time, the Welsh-speaking lads often sat next to each other, and his first words were that gunshot marriages were more common in Cardiganshire than in any other county. The eyes of all the class were focused on us, as they knew that three of us were from that county. We Cardis got up, made a bow, and everybody clapped as we sat down. It was a hilarious moment.

Another fact that was mentioned was that suicide occurred more often in Dyfed, that is in Cardiganshire, Carmarthenshire and Pembrokeshire per unit population than the whole of the British Isles. He could only suggest reasons, maybe genetic depression, loneliness among farmers with financial difficulties, etc.

I can remember Professor Keith Simpson giving a talk as visiting lecturer. As head of forensic science at Guy's Hospital, he was also pathologist to the Metropolitan Police. His experience was incomparable, and so was his delivery of the subject. I sat next to Bernard Knight, who was a student in the year ahead of me. At the end of the talk, Bernard turned to me and said that the lecture had made him decide to specialise in the subject. In due course, he became professor in the Cardiff Medical School, and bought a summer residence next to my grandmother, Esther, by the church in Llangrannog. Much of his time there was spent writing novels, some based on his wide experience in Cardiff.

It was in this fifth year, just before Christmas, that one of my red-letter days occurred. I had gone back to William Diamond Ward in the CRI where the medical unit was. The house physician was on holiday, and I was asked to take care of a patient who had come in. He was a schoolteacher, and the school had started its holidays, so he didn't miss teaching time. It was an honour to have been asked to do this, with eighteen months to go before qualification. When examining him I relied on my old friend D A's words and teaching, and they did not fail me.

He was a man of thirty-three, and suffered from pain in his tummy, usually on the right side, up near the chest. With a weight loss of 10 lbs in the last three months, he needed investigation, but he was not very ill. There was some vomiting, with an itchy backside. His summer holidays had been spent in Kenya.

A full examination followed, but nothing was found and his blood tests were normal. I gave him a bed pan (what had D A taught me?) and asked him to keep his motions in it until I examined them. This surprised him a little. On the first day there was nothing unusual, but the next day, there was something strange that I had not seen before in man or animal (yes, I was brought up on a farm!). It appeared to look like the tail end of a snake, six inches long, segmented, with the segments attached to one another; not alive. I went to the kitchen, where I found an old jam pot and placed the specimen in it, covered in water to stop it drying out and sealed it with a lid.

Where did we go from here? It was obvious. I went to the pathology museum where there were hundreds of specimens kept from years gone by, all labelled. They were preserved in formalin in sealed glass jars. I went through the shelves and after ten minutes I found the answer. It was a tapeworm with the Latin name *taenia saginata*.

I was very pleased with myself and went to show my specimen to my senior doctors on the unit, who agreed with my findings. The next stage was to give the teacher some poison, enough to kill what was left of the worm in the bowel, but not enough to kill him! This was a drug called Niclosamide, in the form of tablets, to be chewed on an empty stomach. (The worm was eating whatever came through from the stomach, as it was attached to the small bowel.) This was followed in three hours by a cupful of saline solution. Two days later, in the bed pan was a tapeworm, over a foot long. On its head were its four hooks that kept it attached to the bowel wall. It had released its hold after being killed, and through it came, proving the first diagnosis I had made on my own.

The patient was discharged. When he returned to the hospital for a check up he had put on 10 lbs in weight and was pronounced 100 per cent fit. The patient's background history which I had taken on the first day had given me a clue as to what was wrong. Yes, as D A said, "Listen to the patient, he tells you the diagnosis". Ten per cent of Kenyans suffer from tapeworm infestation!

Studying public health taught me how important hygiene is to the general public. Food hygiene is all-important and special attention should always be given to the handling of food. Many an epidemic over the centuries has been caused by lack of hygiene. The *cryptospiridium bacillus* caused a major outbreak of dysentery in north Wales, affecting the population supplied with water from Llyn Cwellyn. How did the bug get into the water? Was somebody 'caught short', carrying the bug, and it entered the supply? We have never been informed who or what was responsible.

The professor gave a lecture on epidemics in Croydon, cholera in 1831 and typhoid in 1936. On both occasions the water supply was to blame. Without knowing, one of the workers was a carrier. He was too lazy to come to the surface to pass water and urinated where he was working: the product entered the pipes. Medical tests showed who was responsible, and he later confessed.

A similar occurrence happened a few years ago in London at a meeting of the Royal College of Physicians. In the evening, there was a dinner for the consultants and their wives at a top hotel. The sweet was raspberry fool and ice cream. In a few weeks scores of those who had attended became ill and jaundiced, with four of the wives being at death's door.

Investigations proved that it was hepatitis B, much worse than hepatitis A, originating where the raspberries came from, the famous fruit farms of Blairgowrie in Scotland. All the workers were tested, and one was a carrier of the disease, later confessing his sins. Had he worn his trousers the same way as the vicar wears his collar, this would not have happened!

When the exams came, my written work was satisfactory but I was worried about the oral tests. My examiners in the viva were the professor and Dr Bevan, Chief Medical Officer for Cardiff. Did he know my background, or did I enter the room like a farmer would? Most of my questions were on milk, and as I chatted too much, the professor did not get a word in. He asked how milk was pasteurised, at what temperature and for how long. Then he asked about TB in cattle, and how did man get infected from this source. There are five varieties of the *tuburcle bacillus*: the human variety being one; another is the bovine. Interestingly, one infects voles only. To be honest, I forget the other two! Badgers were mentioned – were they involved? Post mortems on these creatures showed a lot of tuberculosis. What was 'tuberculin tested'? I'd seen this being done on the cattle at home. Brucellosis was discussed, which was easy for me because we had an epidemic in the herd in the 1940s and suffered great financial loss. The cows aborted mid-pregnancy with severe loss of milk and there were no calves to breed or sell. All this was for me part of my experience on the farm and I was lucky and passing the exam was a formality.

St David's Hospital was my location for midwifery experience as a doctor. One thing I remember is that at one time in the antenatal ward we had a mother aged forty-seven and her daughter of twenty-two in beds next to each other – the mother and daughter delivering the same time. We called the older one 'Gran'!

All students had to deliver twenty babies each, all uncomplicated. Difficult births were dealt with by the qualified obstetricians, the house surgeon at the time being the late Dr John Hughes from Aberystwyth and the SHO, Dr Eleanor Hughes, his wife. Yes, this is where they met, probably over a bed, delivering a baby!

Holidays were a welcome break from the hospital and walking was important to me when I was home on holiday. I had to study for much of the time and took a break by walking to Maesllyn. This meant passing five houses, one of which was Panteg where Tomos Lewis, a colourful character lived. He was a pipe smoker, and the whole house reeked of tobacco. He was in his eighties and lived on a small pension, finding it difficult with the price of tobacco going up each year. Eventually, he used to say, his only pleasure was to light the pipe and put it out as quickly as he could!

He was an observant and intelligent man. Calling in to see him and listening to his humorous stories added pleasure to the walk. One day before I returned to my final year as a student, he told me of two medical students, both in their final year walking along the road, when they met an elderly gentleman coming towards them. His features showed the signs of ageing. He stooped and his legs were as stiff and straight as two posts, straight and close together. He stopped to talk to the students, and one of them said that they had been discussing what could be wrong with him. "What do you think?" asked the old man. The first said osteoarthritis, the second thought a disease of the nervous system. "Both wrong" he said, "I'm desperate to go to the toilet!"

In my final year, I studied hard every night. Swallowing textbooks was my priority, ready to be regurgitated when necessary in the examinations!

Surgery was my great passion. In the final exam, the written paper went well, indeed, very well. Next was the practical exam where the student was given a patient and asked to examine him or her and give the diagnosis, and answer questions from the professor. I went to Llanbradach Ward, where the patients were all women, all in bed waiting and being paid for their time if they were not in-patients. "Go to the fourth bed on the left", was the direction. I went with a nurse in attendance.

Here I found a young lady of twenty-two, a secretary, who had been unwell for three months, was losing weight, although she was eating well. She was tired, nervous and perspiring more than usual, preferring colder weather. Her heart raced at times, she also had some diarrhoea and irregular periods.

Examination revealed that her eyes were more prominent than usual, but no double vision. By now, I had some idea what the diagnosis was. The tremor in her hands was more visible when I put a sheet of paper over her outstretched fingers. Her pulse rate was 90 per minute (normal is 70). The neck showed a swollen thyroid gland, generally, but nothing localised. My diagnosis was *thyrotoxicosis* – an overactive thyroid.

The time came to present my case to Professor Lambert Rogers, an Australian by birth. He asked me what was wrong with her. I replied, "Parry's Disease, later known as Graves Disease, named after a London physician, Sir Robert Graves. Graves described it in 1874, but Parry, Caleb Hillier Parry, had described it with a classic paper in 1825, almost half a century before." Parry was of Welsh stock, and later became physician in the Bath General Hospital. I told the professor that Parry had been wronged by not having the disease named after him. Graves was knighted but Parry was forgotten. The professor said that he was glad to learn something he had not known before! A discussion of the treatment for the disease followed.

When the results came, there was a star opposite my name to say distinction, but also another with a gold medal to announce that I was top surgeon of my year out of sixty students. I was the happiest person in the world.

BRAIN SURGERY

IT WAS THE 31ST of July 1956, and I had just arrived in Cardiff on my way back from west Wales, and decided to walk to the hospital. Going through Howells, the famous store, I saw a notice, 'Three shirts for the price of two!' As a Cardi, how could I resist a bargain? My superiors always wore white shirts, and I thought, although I had not reached their status, at least I could look like them!

Off I went to the hospital with my case and plastic bag containing my bargain. As I went through the front door, I noticed a new porter. "Which ward?" he said. It was my pleasure to say that I was a new doctor, not a patient. Ever after, whenever he saw me, the porter would greet me with "Which ward today, Doc?"

During supper time I mixed with new doctors and those that had been there for the past twelve months. The difference was obvious – those that had been there looked tired and pale from hard work and lack of sunshine, because they spent most of the time indoors.

My first post was as house surgeon to the man who had given me a gold medal, Professor Lambert Rogers. He had three housemen: one had to work for Mr Charles Langmaid, the consultant neurosurgeon for two of the six months, doing brain surgery, and I was chosen to do this. As a student, I had never seen a brain operation, but here I was and I had no choice but to get on with it.

At around 10 o'clock that night, before going to bed, I went round the neurosurgical patients on the ward to get some idea of what was going on and, much to my surprise, who was there but Mr Langmaid himself. He asked who I was, and I could see by his facial expression that he was surprised at my keenness. No words were said.

All was quiet on my first morning. Mr Langmaid and Mr

Jennett, the registrar, were in the theatre operating. At 12.30 p.m., there was a phone call notifying us that a patient was on her way down from Pontypool, with a brain haemorrhage. She was 22 years old. I went for an early lunch so that I would be ready when she arrived. A call came from the ward at 1.40 p.m. – she had arrived. I went immediately to William James Thomas Ward, and in the first bed on the right, sitting up, was a beautiful girl with natural blonde, curly hair. Her parents were with her. I asked the nurse to take them to the kitchen and give them a cup of tea while I took the history, and to return as my chaperon when examining the patient afterwards.

When I examined her she showed no abnormality, not even a stiff neck. She sat up, was fully conscious and talked normally to us. She said that she had got up at half past seven that morning to go to work, but she suddenly had a severe headache. This was so severe it made her vomit. She had gone back to bed because the headache was so bad. Her doctor came and she was taken to the local hospital where a lumbar puncture revealed blood in the fluid that circulates around the brain and spinal cord.

Even with my lack of experience, I knew the seriousness of the situation, and asked the nurse to stay with her while I spoke to her parents. I told them that she was seriously ill despite the fact that she felt better and seemed normal. I told them that anything could happen at any moment, and that further tests would be carried out including injecting a dye into an artery in the neck which would reach the brain. X-rays would reveal the leaking artery, and we would probably carry out brain surgery to try to remedy the condition.

After speaking to the parents, I returned to the ward straightaway, and the nurse said she thought the patient had gone to sleep. I examined her. She was not breathing; there was no heartbeat. The beautiful young woman was dead. What a tragedy. The artery that had burst in the morning had bled further, so much so that it had killed her. Thank goodness I had stressed the serious nature of the illness to her parents.

I went to see them immediately. When I told them the tragic news they were brave and sensible, but must have been heartbroken.

I went down to theatre to explain to my superiors what had happened: they were having a sandwich between an operation in the morning and another in the afternoon. Brain operations usually lasted four to five hours. When I told them what had happened, they said little, because death was a daily part of their lives and they had seen it all before. However, the death of a young person who had all her life in front of her – my first patient to die – was a great shock to me.

The tragedy of that young woman's death has stayed with me all my life. It showed me how fragile life is, and that death can come at any moment to the young and old alike. It made me realise that I must strive to achieve the highest standards possible to save as many lives as I could – even though there would be those like this woman, whose lives I would be unable to save. I vowed that I would always do the best for my patients, and that the three words, care, caring and careful would be my motto as a doctor.

A brain haemorrhage is usually lethal, however there are many who survive to live to a ripe old age. Mervyn Davies, one of Wales's greatest rugby players, suffered a brain haemorrhage while playing an international match in the Arms Park in the late 1970s. He was treated successfully on the same unit as I worked in.

After that tragic start to my work as a doctor, the first month went by reasonably well. I worked day and night – twenty-four hours a day for thirty-one days without one hour off, caring for patients with brain and spinal cord conditions, and often doing five or six lumbar punctures in a morning. On the 1st of September, when I looked in my pigeonhole, there was a brown envelope. In it, my pay for August. Having worked all those hours – and for less than £20!

We also had to do casualty work, once every ten days, starting at 5 p.m. until midnight, in addition to our appointed job. Another person followed from midnight to 8 a.m. I remember Christmas Eve, 1956, when it was my turn, and between 5 p.m. and midnight, I saw eighty-four patients. Bed was a wonderful place that night! A young doctor's hours are often unreasonable, and as many as 25 per cent of doctors in their first year show signs of depression.

It was work that kept one on one's toes with the adrenalin pumping. There were all kinds of emergencies, and some not emergencies. Policemen were frequent visitors to the casualty department, questioning patients, usually after car accidents, and usually due to an excess of alcohol. Saturday afternoons saw an increase in sports injuries, and the first doctor on duty from noon to midnight had a rough time.

It was not all hard work and tragedy, however, and there were times of pure comedy. One of the strangest cases I had as a young doctor was a man of forty, white skinned, looking very nervous who asked to see a male doctor. He could not sit, and refused to tell the sister what the trouble was. Suspecting venereal disease, she put him in a room on his own. On entering, he refused to answer my questions, but seeing I was a sympathetic doctor he eventually dropped his trousers.

There, at the entrance, or exit, to or from his bottom was the metal end of a light bulb! Having never seen or heard of such a thing before, what was I to do? The muscles around the opening were in tension, making the problem worse. I started by giving him a quick acting tranquilliser to relax his mind. He found it difficult to understand why a tablet by mouth would help the other end! After a quarter of an hour, I put on my rubber gloves, and I used half a jar of a greasy ointment around the 'foreign body'. I even got some into a large syringe and squirted it past the bulb. With tender loving care I started manipulating the offending object, thinking all the time, what if it breaks? The job would be a hundred times more difficult, with a general anaesthetic needed and having to remove all the broken glass. Gradually, talking all the time in order to relax him, I had the whole bulb in my rubber glove. If you must know, it was a 60-watt **OSRAM!**

Returning to the doctors' residence, I told my colleagues who were watching TV what had happened. One wag in the corner of the room asked, "Was the light on or off?" It was that kind of wit that often kept us going through the gravity of many a situation. After the patient left casualty for home, I thought to myself – where was his real problem, head or bottom?

I was enjoying doing brain surgery. It was a Wednesday in September, and I'd had a reasonably quiet day and was looking forward to reading in my room, a novel maybe, but at 5.30 p.m. there was an urgent call to the accident department. There was a boy of eleven who had been knocked down by a lorry and was unconscious. A full examination revealed a bruise on his right forehead and little else, but observing the golden rule – 'Never leave an unconscious person' – I stayed with him and after five minutes his condition had deteriorated. He was sinking deeper and deeper into unconsciousness.

The main sign of his injury was an enlarged right pupil. In accidents to the head, such as on sports fields or knockouts in boxing, the eyes are an all-important clue. It is the size of the pupils, and differences between the right pupil and the left that are observed by the experts. The child's right pupil was enlarging quickly and there was no time to lose if we were to save his life and prevent irreparable brain damage.

I rang Mr Langmaid and Mr Jennett to come in quickly. Two police cars answered the emergency call and led them through the rush-hour traffic. By the time they arrived, I had the boy in theatre, his head completely shaved and lying on his left side so that the right side of his skull was facing up ready to operate.

Mr Langmaid opened the skull above the right ear, much more crudely than normal due to the urgency – it was life or death. Blood was found inside, lots of it, but finding the source of bleeding was difficult. He took an hour to find it – every time he came near the source of the bleeding more blood would flow, hiding it again. I had organised two pints of blood to transfuse if necessary – we used four! After stopping the bleeding, the pressure in the skull had decreased, and one could see the pupil decreasing in size, and eventually after two hours, it was back to normal.

After the operation as much bone as had been kept from the urgent entry into the skull was replaced, and the skin sutured, with the usual dressing over the lot. The eye had returned to its normal size by now.

My duty was to observe post-operative progress, continuously of course, but at 10 p.m., Mr Langmaid came in from his home and told me the patient would be fine and that I could go to bed. By then, I was pleased that I had made the correct diagnosis, my first ever. If we had left it for another hour he would have died.

The boy walked out after ten days, a healthy normal child. The only difference was a squint of the right eye – a small price to pay for saving his life. I had experienced the drama of a life or death emergency, but more importantly had saved a child's life.

The work was endless, night and day. After two months, I should have moved to the surgical unit proper with Professor Lambert Rogers, doing general surgery. However, Mr Langmaid and the registrar had not had a holiday, so in order that they could each have a fortnight's holiday, I had to stay on for a further month. This meant that I had to assist with every major operation, even closing the huge wounds that had been caused by getting into the brain through the skull. The fact that the brain is so soft means it has to be well protected and this, of course, is provided by a bony skull, but there are problems, the main being that it is much harder gaining entry when things go wrong.

What surprised me most during my time doing brain surgery was the method used to get through the bone in order to remove a disc of about 6 inches in diameter. Five holes were made in a circle, with a brace and bit, exactly the same as I had used in woodwork at school. Then, a wire-saw like the one used to cut cheese was passed down the hole, along the inside and up through the next opening. A handle was attached to both ends, and the wire pulled back and forth until it had cut through the bone – how crude. Today, an electric bit holder is used which halves the time to gain entry. When stitching it all back, Mr Langmaid would start at one end with myself the other. On the last day, Mr Langmaid allowed me do an operation myself. I'm glad to say that the patient survived and was never told who performed her operation!

Work was continuous, night and day, but I was allowed out of the hospital twice in the three months, both times during October. The first was to listen to Mr Langmaid accompanying Leon Goosens, the country's most famous oboist at the time, in a concert lasting over two hours. His ability as a surgeon was obvious, but I did not know of his expertise as a pianist. He was the organist at his local church for many years, and the concert was held there.

The second outing was when I was invited to dinner with Mr Langmaid's family on a Sunday evening. He came to fetch me and brought me back after the feast. During the evening, music from the record player was continuous, and I was asked to pass Mr Langmaid one of the PVC long playing records. I handled the record incorrectly and my thumb left a mark on the surface! That was the only telling off I had from him – in the three months I worked with him he had found no fault with my surgical work!

I wasn't ever thanked for my long hours and diligent effort: it was expected. The pay was grim but, looking back, it was a great experience that I will never forget.

Why didn't I proceed with a career as a surgeon? That is a question my friends and family have always asked me. I have never answered them honestly. However, this is the time to state why I didn't proceed with that speciality. Everybody, including the professor, expected me to become a surgeon. I had won the gold medal for surgery and they were impressed by my work and had perfect confidence in me. One day, something happened that I have never mentioned until now. Once a week, at 8 o'clock in the morning, about twenty specialists would show the most interesting cases to each other. The professor had asked me to show one of our patients to these people. I started well, but then after three minutes I started stammering. Indeed, the stammering became so bad that I had to stop. There was silence and then the professor took my place. I was humiliated in front of all those important people and in my own mind I had failed. I have relived those awful moments many times in my life. I had the skill and knowledge but I was unable to talk publicly and this was an important part of a top surgeon's life.

Strangely enough, none of the doctors ever mentioned the incident to me, and I was given no sympathy or advice. I have kept the incident locked up in my mind until now, and it is a relief to speak of it at last.

DIAGNOSIS – FALSE AND TRUE

THE NEXT THREE MONTHS were spent as house surgeon with Professor Lambert Rogers, dealing with all aspects of surgery other than the brain. Professor Rogers was a man of habit, and his routine was a fixed one which we all had to follow. I was required in my role to have my breakfast early, before eight, and then proceed around the wards to find out what had happened overnight. I was then to knock on Professor Rogers's door at exactly 8.30 a.m. to report to him personally. His Rolls Royce was always parked by the hospital's front door.

On my first day, I was told to look after the male patients on Elize Nixon Ward. The sister had recently been appointed, and in fact, she had been staff nurse on Mametz Ward when I was a student – and had not forgotten me. I helped her with a female patient who was grossly overweight and had been operated on for a bowel problem. She could not pass water, and the bladder was getting bigger and bigger. Sister had tried to catheterise her, but failed. Too embarrassed to tell anyone, she asked me to help. I had never done one before. On went the rubber gloves, size 8. I succeeded, and a large amount of urine was collected, about 2 litres, with the container having to be emptied and replaced.

When the early morning rush was over the sister took me around, starting in a small two-bedder on the right near the entrance to the ward and the sister's office. Much to my surprise, it was occupied by two elderly women. It was there that the professor kept his VIPs. Behind a screen, next to the door, was Mrs Evans, and we were introduced. She was 80 years old from Cardiff, originally from Aberystwyth. The most obvious finding was her skin, which was jaundiced, and as yellow as a gold sovereign. I would have to spend half an hour chatting to her, so I decided to see her last, and briefly get to know the others.

After a cup of coffee with the sister, I went back to Mrs Evans. She was the mother of the previous sister, who had just retired to look after her at home. She had seen the professor a few days previously. He was always very kind to staff and their relatives. He had told her that he was very sorry that she had cancer, probably of the stomach and spreading to the liver, but that she could stay on his ward for the rest of her days, with her daughter visiting whenever she wanted to. No investigations were done, because his word was law.

Sister and I were not happy with this, and we took it upon ourselves to look into her case more thoroughly. So, we went back to basics, using a bed pan and keeping the motions and urine for examination. The motions were almost white, like putty and the urine was dark brown, caused by the bile collecting in her system, and excreted through the kidneys instead of into the bowel.

After four days, Mrs Evans said the pain in her tummy had disappeared and she felt like eating. A miracle? The professor was very religious, and read the lesson in the Sunday service in the church attached to the hospital. His deputy, Mr Aldis, was a lay preacher as well as an excellent surgeon, and I never went to his room without seeing his Bible being open on his desk. Had their prayers influenced her illness? Sister and I were at a loss as to what had happened. After a further three days, we noticed the colour of the motion turning brown, and the urine becoming paler. A visit to the bed pan in the sluice revealed the answer – a large gallstone, one inch in diameter, had been blocking the bile from coming down from the liver and had released itself.

What were we going to tell the professor? The truth always stands, so, we ventured to tell him. He was very humble and congratulated us. From then he always asked our opinion on every diagnosis, "What do you think, Elias?" After a week she was allowed home, and all that was needed was good food to return her to good health. Her daughter visited the ward after some weeks and was grateful to us for making the correct diagnosis and curing her mother.

One of the male patients on the big Elize Nixon Ward taught me and others my senior so much about being a doctor. This story shows how even an experienced doctor can be led astray. We are all human, and make mistakes – the fewer the better! He was fifty-five, and had been sent in by his GP with a provisional diagnosis of cancer of the stomach. He was a native of north-west Wales, where he had lived all his life until four years prior to admission.

The day before the patient was due to go to theatre for his operation I went to see him. It seemed a classical case of cancer of the stomach, pain in the right place, weight loss, loss of appetite, etc. The X-rays showed a roughening of the stomach lining, but nothing definite. The professor said – and his word was law – that we must operate. I happened to be assisting that day. The tummy was opened down to the stomach with a three-inch incision to gain entry. No abnormality was found. All the other organs, pancreas, liver and spleen were examined, but all was well. We had to face the facts. There was nothing physically wrong with the patient. These were the days before cameras to look down into the stomach through the mouth and gullet, which would have saved us from having to perform this traumatic procedure.

After he regained consciousness, I had to tell him the truth. He wouldn't believe me, but after a quarter of an hour of insisting I was right, he was convinced. I returned to him the next day to question him, and to analyse his mind! It became clear that he was depressed, but had masked it and had cancerophobia. Three months previously, he had read a book on the symptoms of stomach cancer, and had convinced himself it could be nothing else but cancer.

A Welsh *englyn*, written by Isfoel, my grandmother's brother, speaks of the importance of the mind in medicine:

The Doctor

His bottle cured Betty – his advice
Was enough for Mary,
Seeing him was enough for Davy,
Mind was the trouble of all three.

Maybe the blacksmith, farmer and bard from Llangrannog, knew more than the specialists who had studied medicine for years!

A big day in my life occurred in the November. On a Saturday afternoon when I was on duty in my white coat, a message came from the porter at the front lodge that some members of my family had arrived to see me. When I went down, who was there but my father and youngest brother, Elwyn. He had been representing his school, Ardwyn, Aberystwyth, in a schools quiz at the BBC studios. I could not leave the hospital because I was on call so I took them for a cup of tea and a tour of the hospital wards and theatres. Elwyn was in the sixth form, studying English, Welsh and History.

After taking him round he was obviously fascinated and I asked him, "What about studying medicine?" To my complete surprise he said, "Yes"! His conversion to medicine was as sudden as Paul's on the road to Damascus.

When he returned to school on the Monday he asked the headmaster if he could switch from studying arts subjects to doing science. The headmaster was reluctant to agree because he was already halfway through his first term, but Elwyn was adamant. The teachers were sceptical, in fact, the physics master commented "You haven't a hope of passing – starting the course at this late stage!"

Elwyn passed his exams with flying colours and went to Guy's Medical School. He went to the Royal Free Hospital as a lecturer with Dame Sheila Sherlock, the world authority on liver disease at the time. His next move was associate professor in Yale Medical School in the USA, and then back to Birmingham to open a new liver unit, performing liver transplants. Within ten years, it was the biggest in Europe, with forty-three beds. He became president of the British Gastro-Enterology Society, and now travels all over the world lecturing, and was recently visiting professor of medicine to the Australian College of Physicians. Who could have predicted that a guided tour of a hospital could have such an effect?

I learnt early in my professional career that being humble and talking to everybody was a great asset. Everybody has something to say, usually worth listening to. Often the ward sister has information that is crucial for the diagnosis and well-being of a patient. I found that porters too knew more than was thought, and their dark humour lightened many a day.

There was a man of fifty on Elize Nixon with a minor complaint. His big toenail, growing like a sheep's horn, needed removing under local anaesthetic, a very minor operation of around ten minutes. He was unemployed and was admitted in order to show the students his condition. He was a nervous character and when the day came for him to have his operation the porter arrived with a wheelchair and a piece of paper. Pretending to read it, the porter said, "Mr Thomas?"

"Yes" said the patient.

"Amputation of the right leg."

Mr Nelson almost fainted. "No, no, no," he said.

"But", said the porter, "that's what's on the paper, and I have good news for you. A patient on the other ward is having his left leg amputated and wears the same size shoes – he is willing to buy your right slipper"! Eventually the patient realised that the porter was pulling his leg and had a good laugh with him and went happily to theatre for his procedure.

The professor kept him in for a further week. This would not have happened today, in fact, he would not have come to the ward at all, but would have been an outpatient, with the practice nurse doing the dressings at home. Speed is everything now, turning the patient out almost before he enters the hospital. Statistics have become so important, with records made of the hours spent in care, and if these are not satisfactory, the health departments get on their high horse. Figures have become more important than the patient.

There was quite a lot of teasing and leg pulling and I was once the victim. I was performing my first toenail removal operation one day, and there was a drop of blood on the dressing. The registrar popped in to see if all was well and commented, "How many pints of blood have you ordered?"

Success and Failure

A DAY OR TWO after New Year's Day, 1957, before finishing my stint with Professor Lambert Rogers, I was asked by Professor Scarborough to be his house physician. It was he who had given me my first lecture as a medical student. It was the most prestigious appointment in Wales at that level. I would be working in the medical unit where the most complicated problems were dealt with.

In my first week, a young man, John Roberts, aged seventeen, arrived at 3.00 p.m. from Brynsiencyn in Anglesey. He had travelled by car because he was not ill enough to warrant an ambulance. He was a Welsh-speaker who had been to Bangor Hospital twice, Liverpool Infirmary twice and Manchester once, but with no diagnosis or treatment. Because of his strong north Walian accent, the registrar asked me to take his history and examine him. He was sitting on the edge of the bed, with his cup of tea, and I greeted him in his native tongue.

We got on well, and I obtained a good medical history, which normally leads one to the correct diagnosis in over 90 per cent of cases. The main symptom was pain in his upper tummy, between the navel and chest bone, which he had suffered, off and on, since the age of ten. It came on when he ate, and nothing eased it but time. As the stomach emptied – in one to two hours – he would feel better. I asked every question that seemed relevant, without a clue to the answer to his problem. To me, the condition was definitely physical, although he had been told in the other hospitals that it was "All in the mind!" All I knew was that there was something wrong in the stomach or nearby. Investigations elsewhere, including several barium meal X-rays, were normal.

He was very emaciated and weighed just over 5 stone and was 5 feet 4 inches tall. His ribs protruded like photographs

Winning a beauty contest at the age of four

Hefin and I in the bathtub

Dyfed and Dilys

My father and mother

My foster family – Aunt Annie, Uncle Evan and Aunt Lisa

The Alltycnydau farmyard and kitchen

With Aunt Annie

The Gold Medal for Surgery

Ken Lane – my heart
transplant patient

Pam Jones who
stopped smoking
through hypnosis

Colin Ballett who had a heart attack at a petrol station

Lifesaving 'miracle'

By Ian Bebb

A MIRACULOUS coincidence may have saved the life of a Penarth man who collapsed at a garage – after an ambulance took more than half an hour to respond to the emergency call.

Seventy-three-year-old Colin Ballett, who has a serious heart condition, was left fighting ofr his life after collapsing at the Penarth Tesco garage.

According to his wife Simone, Colin owes his survival to the fact that retired GP Dr Joshua Elias – once Colin's own doctor at Stanwell Road Surgery – was in the garage filling up his car with petrol at the time.

Colin, of Penarth Marina, collapsed when his pulse rate soared to 255 as he stopped at the garage on New Year's Eve.

Simone said: "I feel that Dr Elias,

who by a miracle happened to be at the garage that day, was instrumental in keeping my husband alive in a life-threatening situation.

"I thank God daily for him being there.

"We explained clearly when we made the emergency call that it was a life-threatening situation, but after 30 minutes there was still no sign of an ambulance.

"We were on the point of making a third emergency call when it arrived – apparently from Cowbridge."

When the ambulance finally arrived, Simone said the crew would not use a defibrillator to assist her husband – explaining he would have to wait for hospital staff to apply it.

Simone said: "I just can't under-

stand why they wouldn't use the defibrillator.

"I really would like to know if it's because the staff weren't trained to use the equipment or if it's ambulance trust policy not to use them."

Dr Joshua Elias said: "I asked for a defibrillator to come with the ambulance. Colin had gone into what we call orricular fibrillation with his pulse rate over 200.

"He was very ill and could have died on the spot.

"I certainly think it would help if all ambulance drivers were able to use defibrillators on the spot, with prior consent of hospitals."

Colin, a former British Telecom worker, is now in a stable condition in Llandough Hospital and is awaiting tests to find out more about his condition.

Simone added: "I would like to express my heartfelt gratitude for the concern and kindness shown by the staff at Tesco – in particular customer services manager Maria and store manager Trevor.

"Since New Year's Eve we have received phone calls, fruit and flowers from Tesco – which is not a faceless giant, but a store with compassionate, caring people."

The Welsh Ambulance Services NHS Trust refused to comment on the use of defibrillators by ambulance crews.

In a statement a spokesperson said: "The Welsh Ambulance Services NHS Trust has not received a complaint from the patient or the patient's family. Should the Trust do so it will ensure that the matter is looked into accordingly."

The report about Colin Ballett in the *Penarth Times*

John Roberts
(second from right)
at the age of fifteen

John Roberts three years
after his operation

Janet completing the London Marathon in six days in 2005

With Professor John
Dodge

Kate Dodge

Dr Myrddin Evans

On a cruise with my wife Jo

My two sons, Ian and Marc

Hefin

Dyfed

Dilys

Elwyn

Amy, Ian's daughter at the age of eight

Rhian, Marc's daughter at the age of eight

George Joshua, my grandson at the age of six

of inmates in Belsen Concentration Camp. I went through every system thoroughly, but could find nothing except a little tenderness in the stomach area. Several consultants saw him, but were unable to offer an answer.

We then asked one of Wales's top surgeons, Mr Foster, for advice. He arrived with his entourage, and with about twelve doctors of all grades around John's bed, perused his notes thoroughly. Then, after a short examination, as everybody else's fingers had been feeling for clues, he decided he could not let him go back home without solving the dilemma. He would operate on him as soon as possible.

I had to inform the parents and ask for permission. There wasn't a phone in the house, so it had to be done via the family doctor. They arrived in a couple of days, grateful that something was being done to alleviate their son's pain at last. Why hadn't the specialists from other hospitals in England and Wales tried harder to cure him?

He was placed on a long list of operations for the following Monday, indeed, the first, for 8.00 a.m. I had taken blood from him the night before for cross matching should he need a transfusion, due to possible blood loss.

There was too much to do on the ward for me to go to theatre to see the operation and get the diagnosis, but like a bush telegraph, the answer arrived by 10.00 a.m. The stomach was normal, with an opening and exit as it should be, but next to it was a smaller one, the size of a small orange or tangerine. This smaller stomach was closed with no entry or exit from it. It was under the same influence as the normal stomach so that as the lad ate, juices were formed in both, but there was no way for them to escape from the little stomach, and therefore pressure built up causing pain. The fluids would gradually be reabsorbed into the system as the food left the normal stomach.

The small extra stomach was removed completely and his pain disappeared. He returned to Brynsiencyn a pain-free and happy man. When I saw him twelve months later, he had gained two stone in weight and two inches in height. By now he was 18 years old and able to work every day as a garage mechanic in Menai Bridge.

Despite fifty years having gone by almost to the day to the writing this book, I decided to try to find out how John had got on in life. My method was to get the phone number of each Roberts in the village of Brynsiencyn (there were eleven), and start ringing. The first two had not heard of him, but the third said, "Jack Roberts here". I told him my quest, and he said his father had told him about this young man, and was the person who had taken him in his car to the hospitals in Liverpool and Manchester when he was in his teens. His final words were, "I will find him for you".

Three nights later my phone rang and someone said, "John Roberts here. Are you looking for me?" This was him. He had married and moved to Llwynhendy near Llanelli, and had not been ill since his operation. He has four children, and he has worked all his life without losing a day. His life since the operation has been pain free.

At the end of the sixth year, the examinations were held for students with practical exams on the wards. There were ten students on William Diamond, the medical unit ward. I was not allowed to help, but I usually went around to ask, "Everything OK?" A Welsh student I knew from the year behind me in college was there, who told me that her patient had Hodgkin's Disease, but she could not understand his severe itching. All I said was, "Ask him how much alcohol he drinks!" It clicked, the Hodgkin's Disease was affecting the liver, and alcohol was making things worse, causing itching. She passed. In 2005, she was having a cup of tea with her husband and son in the Millennium Centre. I recognised her, shook her hand and said, "Hello". She introduced me to her husband and son and reminded me of the way I had steered her to the right diagnosis.

Before I left the medical unit, two patients influenced my thinking for the rest of my career. The curing of John Roberts was a success story, but these were the opposite. Life is full of ups and downs in the medical profession.

I decided, when I started my work, that an easy way out when dealing with a dying patient or one that suffered from a mortal disease, was to tell them until the end, "You are getting better", or "You will be better tomorrow". What is better than hope for a sick person?

A man of forty-two walked into William Diamond Ward in April. He was very pale. He was given the sixth bed on the right, and after he had settled in, my job was to take his history, examine him and investigate. It became obvious that he had a blood disease, with a large spleen and he bruised easily. Blood tests showed he had leukaemia. There was no treatment in those days. I felt if I told him, it would be as good as giving him his death certificate. He was an intelligent man and married with two young sons, aged twelve and ten. It was a situation I had not dealt with before, and eye to eye contact was difficult.

The next day he asked me, "May I speak to you?" I said I would come back in half an hour. This was not because I was busy: it was to prepare myself for what was coming. Returning, I pulled the screen around the bed, and sat by him. He asked what the trouble was. He said that he owned a garage, and if it was a fatal illness he wished to know so that he could put the business in his sons' names and, if one of them was interested in taking it over when older, they could do so. His chief mechanic would look after things until then.

I didn't have a choice. He was unemotional, sensible, and I told him that he had two months to live. He was grateful and left that afternoon to see his solicitor. It was a difficult situation for me, but he made it so much easier with his practical and brave attitude.

The second case was a blacksmith from rural Pembrokeshire. One of the registrars from the CRI went to work in Haverfordwest General Hospital as a specialist because they had failed to get a locum consultant. This man of fifty-six had been in hospital for a month with diarrhoea. Nobody could make a diagnosis, and no medication helped. So, the specialist brought him back to William Diamond Ward to get more opinions.

The history was brief: diarrhoea for a month. Examination did not help, neither did medicines of any kind. This was very disappointing for the patient and the doctors. I spent much time with him, questioning and re-examining, but to no avail. I was unable to get to the root of his illness.

After a month on the ward I found he had fluid in his chest, what we call pleural effusion. What was the cause? How did this tie this up with the diarrhoea? It is a rule in medicine that one must not make two diagnoses if possible. The conclusion was that he had TB, which had spread throughout his body. Unfortunately, his personality changed owing to his illness: he became insane and had to be sectioned to the psychiatric hospital, where he died within a fortnight. A post mortem showed that he had TB.

I felt humble. Had I done my best for him? As it happens, there was no treatment then for TB of the bowel, and so he could not be cured. Very often getting the right diagnosis can be so difficult before the cause of an illness becomes obvious.

Running for my Life

A MONTH BEFORE FINISHING my six months with Professor Scarborough, a letter arrived from Dr Eirian Williams, consultant at Haverfordwest Hospital and one of Wales's best physicians. The two of them had met in Portmeirion on a weekend conference and Professor Scarborough had recommended me to be Eirian's next registrar when I finished in CRI. I was only twenty-three, but with a large pay rise, it was worth considering. Eirian had made a big name for himself as an expert on brucellosis, and he wrote the chapter on the subject in *The Oxford Textbook of Medicine*, one of the best books in the medical world. (I am also very proud of the fact that my brother, Elwyn, wrote a chapter on liver disease in that distinguished publication.)

However, I had seen an advert in the *British Medical Journal* for a senior house officer at St David's Hospital, Cardiff, working with my old friend Byron, and also two other consultants, Dr Leonard Howells and Dr Idris Jones. It was difficult to decide between the two jobs, but I chose Cardiff where there were many postgraduate lectures that I could attend to advance my learning.

My first visit around the wards gave me confidence. In bed, next to each other, were two elderly women, both over eighty, and deaf. They had been there so long they almost ran the place. I introduced myself, and after speaking to the second, a voice said, "He can put his slippers under my bed anytime". I had obviously passed the test!

Next morning, in my pigeonhole, there was a letter from my Aunty Annie, having been persuaded by my uncle to write it. My work at CRI had been very busy, and my aunts and uncle had hardly seen me for twelve months. As an SHO, I would have every other weekend off, so Uncle Evan suggested that I should buy a car and that he would contribute £500 towards it. Uncle Evan was a true Christian, who practised what he preached. Of the £225 I had earned in the first year, I had saved £180, the reason being that I never had time off and it was, work, work, and more work! A new Morris 1000 was £700 so, after my first month's pay in St David's, I would have enough for the purchase.

The decision was made, and my uncle ordered the car from the local Valley Services Garage at Llandysul. A phone call was received saying that the car had been delivered. It was black with two doors, GEJ 533. On a free Saturday, the first in September, off I went by train and bus and there, awaiting me in Llandysul, was my first car. The first drive was to see my uncle and aunts of course, four miles up the road. I sounded the horn outside their house and out they came, and we all went to New Quay to celebrate with an ice cream each!

When I returned to Cardiff in my new car I found the ideal spot to park it. In front of the hospital was a large car park, but five yards to the left of the front door was a little corner, just the right size for a Morris 1000, and it was there I parked it, summer and winter. When winter came and I needed antifreeze I went to the dispensary for methylated spirits, where it was used in the hospital to sterilise trays, etc. It was perfect as an antifreeze. Interestingly, alcohol is the basis of the antifreeze used today for windscreen washing liquid.

My most memorable patient, perhaps the most disturbing ever and definitely the most dangerous, was a man of sixty. I was on duty on a Saturday morning, and I had the pleasure of having a house physician with me – a woman from Llanelli. The bed bureau, which was in charge of all the hospital beds in Cardiff sent the patient in. The house physician began taking his history, but he became difficult, saying there was no need for all those questions, that he just wanted treatment and would go home.

Having not met his type before, she withdrew from the conversation and came to see me. I told her to take a break for a coffee, and I took over. I was ready for him. My first words were, if he did not wish to cooperate then he should leave the hospital and go home – we did not have to treat him. His attitude improved. Sister was informed of the situation and told that if there was any further nonsense, could they please call me!

His story was that he had slipped going over a hedge, and that barbed wire had injured his right leg. This, he said, had happened on the Tuesday, four days previously. There was nothing else significant in what he said, but we found out that the address he had given was false, as there was no such street in Cardiff! I became suspicious of him and his history of his complaint.

Having drawn the curtains around us and asked him to remove the pyjama trousers lent to him by the sister (who kept spares for those coming in without), I examined him. He had three sore areas, which contained yellow pus, and his lymph glands were swollen in the groin. His temperature was 102°F, or 39°C, and he looked pale. There was one finding that I found very odd and which made me suspicious: all three sore areas, due to cuts of the skin, were directly over the long vein that goes from the foot to the groin, known anatomically as the long saphenous vein. This was too much of a coincidence for me to accept his version of what had happened, and it seemed to me that the wounds were self-inflicted, maybe with a knife. A blood test was negative for septicaemia; that is, the infection had not reached the blood stream. He was given a penicillin injection.

At breakfast time on the Monday morning, I was listening to the radio and heard a police message that they were looking for a criminal in the Cardiff area. The description fitted the patient on Ward 23. I was convinced by now that he was the wanted man. He had cut his leg in three places and had found a hiding place in a hospital bed, where policemen were unlikely to search for him.

He was a rough character, with a belt around his waist about five inches wide like the girth on a horse's harness, and a buckle as big as a shield. I decided to confront him without any policemen present, and informed the sister of the situation beforehand. I told her to stay in her office, which was four yards from his bed, and to phone the police if there was trouble. I approached him and told him of my doubts about him. His face changed. He was furious and jumped out of bed in his bare feet, grabbed his belt and came for me.

I ran away, past the sister's office. He came after me. I fled down the fire escape to the ground floor and out into the open spaces between blocks of buildings, then turned left to the front of the hospital next to Cowbridge Road. By now, the sister had dialled 999 and as we reached the front near the road, I could hear police cars with their sirens ringing. Never have I been so pleased to see police officers! They caught him, handcuffed him and bundled him into their car. His last words, through the car window, to me were, "I'll get you for this!"

After a court hearing, he was jailed for four years for stealing a large sum of money from a Cardiff hotel and with causing grievous bodily harm. I was glad I did not suffer any bodily harm thanks to my youth and my ability to run quickly.

WORKING WITH CHILDREN

A MONTH BEFORE LEAVING St David's Hospital, Dr Percy Bray, Cardiff's top paediatrician, heard that I wanted experience with children. He came to see me and said that he wanted me to spend a year at the East Glamorgan Hospital doing paediatrics. The local paediatrician, or senior hospital medical officer (SHMO), was Dr Bill Davies. I spoke to Bill over the phone and went to meet him and to have a look at the hospital and his department – sixty beds and cots, caring for every kind of illness. The hospital covered a wide area including the Rhondda valleys and Pontypridd, altogether a population of 200,000, with an extra outpatient department in Llwynypia.

After half an hour, Bill told me the job was mine, but I would have to go through an interview with the hospital committee in order to go through the motions of being appointed, but he would be there to make sure they did choose me!

There are various qualifications a doctor can have, the lowest at that time being LMSSA, Licentiate of the Medical and Surgical Society of Apothecaries. I doubt if it still exists. A degree involves an MB, and a higher degree, MD. The short list for the post a few years previously consisted of two people, one with LMSSA after his name, the other with MD, a much higher qualification. The committee, thinking they knew everything, awarded the post to the one with LMSSA because it had more letters than MD! Bill said that he did not want that to happen ever again.

I can remember the post of headmaster of a primary school in Cardiganshire being advertised in the *Western Mail*. The advert said 'Canvassing will disqualify'. It was then usual for the candidate for a post to canvas or go to see each councillor to ask for their backing. Knowing so many people, a local teacher went round some of the councillors to ask for their vote and because he was the best qualified of the candidates he thought he was sure to be successful. He was disappointed not to get the post. He later saw one of the councillors on the appointing committee, a farmer, who told him that he had not voted for him, "Because you didn't come to see me"!

On the 1st of August 1958, I started one of the happiest years of my life, working with children. Children are natural and honest, and I enjoyed every minute of my time working with them. Not only this but the staff at the hospital, the doctors, nurses and cooks, as well as the parents and children, were all wonderful, friendly people. The steaks for lunch were the best ever, and I could have two if I asked. It was the only time in my life I was called 'Sir', having worked in the CRI and St David's in the city, everyone knew me as "Josh". My status was elevated overnight!

Bill's first words stressed the importance of recognising a sick child, or even a very sick child. He emphasised that minutes were important in illnesses that killed quickly, for example, meningitis.

On the first morning, Bill brought a girl of six into a single bedder on Ward 3, who had been ill for a week at home with diarrhoea and vomiting. She was the daughter of an ex-sister of the ward who had left to start a family, and therefore was given VIP status. It was gastro-enteritis, but she had become so dehydrated that a drip had to be put up, and she was fed through a vein, to rest the inflamed stomach and bowels. Having never done this on a child, I was apprehensive, and told Bill so. His response was, "You can do it". The truth was, he had not done one himself for years, and was afraid of trying for fear of failing. All went well, the drip stayed up for five days and by then the girl was drinking and eating without trouble. During the ensuing months, I must have done scores of them.

As the year progressed, before Christmas, I noticed more and more children were coming into the ward with anaemia, as well as their other illnesses. It bothered me, but I knew that this was a poor area, and that it might be a contributory factor. I could not ask Bill because I did not want to show my ignorance. However, one day, one of the boys who was 9 years old, had a haemoglobin count of less than 50 per cent. Haemoglobin carries the oxygen to the body. I did every test to find if he was losing blood through the bowel, kidney, etc. He wasn't. The time had come to ask Bill what was wrong with him! Bill told me to ask the boy where he lived. He told me Taff Street, Pontypridd. That meant nothing to me. Bill then told me to ask him how close to the chip shop he lived. The answer was, "Only ten houses away". Again, I failed to see what this had to do with his illness. Bill told me to ask him how often he went to the chip shop for fish and chips. The answer was, "Every lunch time". "That's the answer" said Bill, "chipanaemia".

His mother would give him sixpence to go to the shop for his lunch. He had no red meat, no iron in his food and the result was anaemia! I had never heard the term 'chipanaemia' before but it is obvious that Bill was acquainted with the condition and had coined the term himself. The boy's mother could not be bothered to cook and it was cheap to send him there. I gave him medicine full of iron and he came back in three months with the haemoglobin count back to normal. I gave his mother a lecture on how to cook a decent lunch for her children, full of liver and red meat!

There is usually one big day in every job, medical or otherwise. This day in the East Glamorgan Hospital was the weekly outpatient session. Bill saw half the patients, and I saw the other half. One day, a mother came through my door with a 7-year-old girl, carrying a letter from the GP saying that the patient was losing weight. She was not eating as she should, and had the occasional pain in her stomach. If she were older, I would suspect an ulcerated stomach or stomach cancer. Her symptoms had been present for six months.

She sat on the couch, with her mother holding her hand. Her eyes were a little pale, maybe anaemic. The only abnormal finding was tenderness in the upper tummy to the left side, with probably a lump, about three inches across in this area, deep down, in or near the stomach. This was definitely not the spleen. I told the mother and informed Bill, who was next door. We decided to admit her immediately, with a view to X-rays after swallowing a little barium the next morning. Mr Melbourne Thomas, the consultant surgeon, gave us his opinion, "There must be some deep seated mischief there", which was his usual comment if he had been unable to make a diagnosis and when action had to be taken.

X-rays showed a 'ball', about three inches across in the stomach. We were puzzled by this because she could not have swallowed something of this size. The surgeon, when he operated on her, found in her stomach a hairy object, looking like a hedgehog, which came out without trouble. All was closed up. Nobody knew what it was.

The hairy object was taken to the laboratory and, under the microscope, one of these prickly hairs turned out to be a coconut fibre. The ball found consisted of scores of them, a mass of coconut fibres. Where had they come from?

Her mother visited in the evening. On questioning, she told me that they had a mat by the front door made of these fibres, and that the girl spent much time there. The girl had been picking the mat, putting the fibres in her mouth and swallowing them. The name for the ball is a bezoar. It is also to be found in animals and requires surgical removal.

By the time the patient returned home she was well. The mother threw the mat into the dustbin. She returned to outpatients in a month, 100 per cent fit, having gained weight and eating well. It is interesting that very often girls with long hair develop this condition, after putting the ends in the mouth, with bits coming off and swallowed, collecting in the stomach.

Half way through my year in East Glamorgan Hospital, I found interest in the psychological effect of hospitalisation on children – a change from the physical! Little, if anything, was known about it until 1952 when Bowlby, a psychologist, wrote his article on the subject for the World Health Organisation in Geneva. My observations regarding this subject were based on a girl of eight who had been on the ward for three months with Still's Disease, which is rheumatoid arthritis in children. Her main treatment was physiotherapy, as medicines were not available for her condition at that time. To my mind, the harmful effect on her mind was far worse than the disease.

She was from Gilfach Goch, some fifteen miles away, and her parents visited once a week, if that. This worried her, and I could see her sadness – there was not a smile on her little face. After a fortnight came despair, she was not eating so well, and not mixing with others. After a further fortnight, she was estranged from her family when they arrived, and showed no interest in them. Sometimes, during this phase, I thought she had got over the sadness, but no. She was quieter, but inside she was suffering more mentally and this could have a permanent effect on her. The psychological effect of being alone in hospital away from her family was much worse than the little improvement achieved by physiotherapy.

This girl was the longest stay patient in the ward, but I kept thinking of others who were in other hospitals for a year or two with orthopaedic conditions or TB, incarcerated and away from family. The effect is frightening, even personality destroying, and is visible having reached adulthood, in the form of obsessive behaviour, depression, etc. How many of you have to walk the same way home always, or check the doors three times to make sure they are locked? Do you have phobias such as being scared of a little spider and having to run to the next room? Many of these psychological problems start with childhood experiences, and often remain with one all through one's life.

One boy of six had pneumonia. He was slow getting better and X-rays revealed a milk tooth down one of the bronchial tubes, obviously inhaled in his sleep. What to do? It had to be removed, and I asked Mr Dilwyn Thomas, chest surgeon at the famous Sully Hospital at the time, to see him. Not wanting to open his chest, he produced a forceps, fifteen inches long, from his bag and told us to sterilise it. The boy was put to sleep and after much effort, the tooth was removed via the larynx and windpipe. Recovery was quick.

East Glamorgan Hospital became famous in 1963 as the last location of smallpox in Great Britain. It shows itself in the form of spots all over the body, and one morning, the consultant gynaecologist to the hospital, Mr Hodkinson, turned up with a spotted forehead. "Look", he said, "My acne is back, after all these years". He was dead in a week. Doctors and nurses were all vaccinated and kept in for six weeks so as not to spread the fatal condition. All patients with smallpox were taken to an isolation hospital at Penrhys, at the top end of the valley, on top of a mountain. They all died.

A great friend of mine, Dr Jimmy Thomas, medical superintendent at St David's Hospital, cared for the unfortunate patients. He had been medical officer in India for several years and had seen much of the horrible disease. He had been vaccinated several times and was immune to the disease. The Queen honoured him with an OBE for his work.

As you are still reading, with the TV turned off and the burning embers ready to disappear or waiting for more wood on the fire, it is worth drawing your attention to an interesting fact and that is, "The tighter the knot holding parents and children close to each other, the easier it is to loosen it when the day comes to leave the nest."

It would be interesting to compare and contrast the minds of children who were separated from their parents during the war, such as evacuees, with those, like west Walians, who were at home throughout the conflict. Also, those who had a difficult time during their childhood, for instance because of the death of a parent or parents, divorces, etc. Is there a difference later in life? I'm sure there is.

At the beginning of this chapter on paediatrics, I mentioned

Dr Percy Bray and must tell you more about him. Trained in the Welsh School of Medicine, he qualified with honours, meaning he had obtained five or more distinctions in the different subjects. The number of doctors who have achieved this are very rare – you can count them with the fingers of one hand. I know of only one, who is now retired and living in Cyncoed. Percy did some of his postgraduate training in London with Archie Norman, and often mentioned his name.

When I worked in Church Village, Percy would come and do the outpatient clinics whilst Bill would go on holidays – some four weeks a year! On his patients' notes, I noticed strange letters on top of the front pages of some, a trio of capitals, PBM, and the others, two which I eventually worked out were Greek, the penultimate one of the Greek alphabet, Psi, followed by Epsilon, written as an 'E'. Having got to know him, I ventured to ask what they meant, and he told me PBM meant poor biological material. That is, the genetic make-up of the patient was not the best. The Greek letters Psi, and Epsilon meant psychosomatic, that is, there was doubt whether much of the illness was mental in origin.

Percy married a girl from west Wales, daughter of the vicar of Trelech, near Newcastle Emlyn. I lost a true friend when he died.

DELIVERING PARCELS OF JOY

I WAS BACK IN Cardiff in August 1959, in the Maternity Hospital, over the road from the CRI, as house surgeon to Professor Archie Duncan. It was quite an honour to have my third professorial house 'job'.

The buildings had an amazing history, starting as eight houses, next to each other, where all the deliveries took place. In the 1930s, a purpose-built hospital was planned, with the metal framework and ground floor completed, but along came the war and it was used as a fire station, which proved very convenient when a bomb struck the infirmary on the worst night of the war for Cardiff, the 3rd of March 1941. The window of the main operating theatre was blown out, the electricity failed and the surgeon had to finish his operation with the sister holding a torch for him. The next day, patients were moved to Whitchurch, Merthyr and Mountain Ash. When the war ended, the steel skeleton became a beautiful building, functional, perfect for obstetrics, and it was a joy to work there for six months.

Above the ground floor were three other floors, A, B and C. A was used by the professor, B by Mr Maliphant and C by Mr Arwyn Evans. The antenatal clinic and research departments were housed on the ground floor. My registrar was Mr Walter Pollard, who became consultant in Bath. He had hands like a farmer, bigger than my uncle's – indeed, more like a lumber jack in the Canadian forests, but his work was excellent.

Walter showed me how to use forceps and off we went, delivering one or two babies by this method most days. My first was unforgettable. Forceps, and out comes the baby, cross-eyed, with ears sticking out like jug handles. I said nothing, and handed him to his mother who said, "Isn't he beautiful?" Yes, the crow sees her young as white! The mother sent me a Christmas card every year until he was ten, with a photograph of her progeny inside, of course.

We dealt with most of the difficult births, but the professor had his 'Fur Coat Clinic', Cardiff's VIPs, who tended to come to him for his expertise. They were university staff, barristers, solicitors, doctors' wives, etc. I had to accompany him during these clinics. It was an education on how to deal with the upper crust, and I held the towel for him every time he washed his hands, of course!

One of the housemen on B floor was quite a character, later a GP in north Wales. His room was full of cases of wine, even though he was only an average drinker. The reason for all the wine bottles was that every birth he assisted, even normal deliveries, but more so with forceps, he used to tell the mothers that they were very difficult and that but for his dexterity and intervention, the result could have been very different. All the mothers believed him, the husbands would be informed and the wine deliveries were almost daily!

About 8 p.m. one evening, I was on duty – we shared night work, with one of the three housemen doing his turn so that the other two could sleep, often having been awake most of the night before. Mr Arwyn Evans, the consultant on C floor, asked me to assist him with a caesarean section operation because one of his friends had gone into labour unexpectedly. He was a wonderful surgeon, so dexterous, and represented Wales at cricket, hockey and one other sport when young. In fact, he went to Switzerland when he was 43 years old to recover from a heart attack, had never played curling before and won the world championship.

He was a wealthy man, and as he was operating he said to me, "What are you doing with your money, Josh?" My answer, which was true, "I haven't any". As a millionaire, he advised me that when I had accumulated a decent sum later in life, I should give it to the family before the Chancellor of the Exchequer got hold of it in death duties. Maybe that is why my cars are getting smaller and my contributions to my chapel in the west aren't increasing! Reading the wills column in the *Daily Telegraph* after he died, he left £14,000. He was a wise man who practised what he preached. The news on the radio was interesting the other day, saying that the biggest savers in Great Britain come from Cardiganshire. Take my advice all you hoarders, give as much as you can afford to the family before the evil day.

On New Year's Day, 1960, a patient came into hospital having been seen in the clinic, and the doctors were not sure if she could have a natural birth. Her waters had broken. The patient was seen by Mr Howard John, a brilliant obstetrician and brother of the famous rugby international player, Roy John from Neath. It was decided to let her try and deliver herself or assist her with forceps, with caesarean section if necessary. She had to be seen every two hours to watch progress, if any, and I was up with her all night. At 6 a.m. I wasn't happy, and rang my registrar, Walter Pollard. The response was, "We will do a caesarean section. I will be in now, and you are doing it." This was a shock to me! I'd been up all night, had worked for almost twenty-four hours and I was expected to perform my first caesarean section. There was no way out. I tried to avoid doing the operation, and all Walter said was, "Get on with it! 'Cometh the hour, cometh the man.'"

In my sterile clothes and rubber gloves, with Walter assisting, I asked the anaesthetist and the sister if they were ready. "Yes" came both answers. The first thing to do was to sterilise the skin of the lower tummy. Next, with a scalpel in my right hand and feeling very nervous, I made the incision from the navel to the pubic bones. The small blood vessels bled, but it was easy to stop the flow. This was followed by cutting through the muscle to expose the womb. Walter showed me the two big arteries that supplied blood to the womb and baby, to be careful not to touch them, and then an incision into the womb.

The baby came out easily, and I asked the sister to hold it as I put two forceps on the middle of the umbilical cord, cutting between them to avoid loss of blood from the baby. Mother and offspring were separate for the first time. The afterbirth came out easily, and all that was left to do was to close the openings I had made in the right order: womb, muscle and then skin. It had taken an hour – not bad for my first caesarian section.

The baby was washed and labelled to prevent a mix-up, with the cord tied with string about three inches from the navel. The mother had regained consciousness by now, and was thrilled to see her baby son, and she was returned to her room when well enough, with her blood pressure being checked for a few hours.

I was tired, having worked continuously for twenty-four hours, but there were another nine hours to go – yes, thirty-three hours non-stop. My visits to mother and baby were frequent during that day, and at 5.00 p.m. off I went to bed, with a phone call to the telephonist that I was not to be awakened until 7.00 a.m. next morning.

After a wash and shave, my first visit before breakfast was to see the mother and baby. All was well and off I went for a celebratory breakfast of ham and eggs. The mother did not know it had been my first caesarian until I informed her when she was leaving for home in Barry. Three further caesarian sections followed before my six months came to an end, all getting progressively easier.

If a doctor disliked working with sick people, it was an excellent speciality, but sometimes, regrettably, the conclusion was different. Sadly, there were about 2 per cent of babies born with physical abnormalities who needed special care.

There was a premature baby ward in the hospital, cared for by Professor Peter Gray, the paediatrician. He knew me, and asked would I look after it while I worked there! Having done a year's paediatrics in East Glamorgan, I couldn't say no. A willing horse gets the most work. One night, when I wasn't on call, the phone rang at 4 a.m. – it was Sister Maggie Auld, the night superintendent, who was later appointed Head of Midwifery for Scotland. One of the babies on the premature unit was born with complete paralysis of one side, a stroke before birth, and was vomiting and getting dehydrated. She thought the baby needed a drip. We discussed the problem, and I felt we should let the baby die, because it was hopeless to expect recovery. However, she insisted, and I proceeded. Professor Gray was in the next day and said he agreed with Sister Auld – a drip was necessary. The baby died five days later.

Ten years later, I was in Llandough Hospital visiting a patient and who saw me but Peter Gray. His words, "Do you remember that baby in Glossop Terrace that night when you thought we should let it die? You were right, and we were wrong." It takes a big man to confess that to someone who was much his junior. We were great friends until he died of cancer of the pancreas. He was a wonderful person.

At a maternity hospital, the main purpose is to get mother and baby (or babies) home in an excellent state of health. I must mention three interesting patients, one of them tragic.

The first case is incredible and stranger than fiction. I was on call at the time and a woman of sixty with grey hair came to the front door of the hospital at ten in the morning. She spoke to the porter first, and asked if she could see a doctor. I went down and led her to a consulting room with a bed if an urgent delivery arrived. We sat down and she informed me that she was pregnant, in fact in labour, and wanted to have the baby there. She was unmarried and childless. All I could see was that she was pushing her tummy forward, as if pregnant. I called for the sister: she had seen two women like this before.

The patient was put on the bed and she told us the baby was coming. She was asked by the sister to push, and I pretended to assist the delivery. When she thought it had come, a big smile appeared on her face and, cleverly, the sister gave her a doll, kept for the purpose. The tummy was now flat. She was left there for a few minutes to enjoy the experience. Soon, she was ready to go home, put on her clothes and refusing a lift, off she went, leaving the doll there. It was a phantom pregnancy, which occurs usually in unmarried women who are childless. I never thought I would see one, but the professor had mentioned it in passing when lecturing to us as students. The human mind is very strange!

The second case was a girl of nineteen from Brecon. She was there one morning when I went to the ward and was told not to ask her any questions. The professor came in later and told me that the father of her baby was the girl's father. This was a sad case of incest. I'd never seen a case like this before. She was moved to Cardiff from the hospital in Brecon as everyone knew her in the area, which made it very difficult for her. Her father was already in jail for the crime, and local papers had been full of the case.

The patient could not maintain eye contact, especially when she realised that I knew. Husbands came to the ward to visit their wives, but nobody visited her. Her delivery was normal, and she returned home the same day. The baby was placed in a Barnado Home.

The third and last case is a tragic event. A local man was walking to work at 7 a.m. one morning, through the lane next to the hospital, when he discovered a dead baby on the floor, clothed in blue knitwear. He came to tell us and we investigated immediately. The news travelled through the hospital like a flash of lightning, and sadness enveloped the whole place. The baby was from C floor, one of the mothers had killed her own baby by throwing the infant out through the window. A psychiatrist was called who removed her to the psychiatric hospital at Whitchurch.

Childbirth is a natural process, physically and mentally, but to some with family or mental problems, difficulties with the father or other relationships, depression, lots of children at home waiting for the mother to return, it can be hell, and that's what happened here. When this is the case, it affects everybody – doctors, midwives, as well as the immediate family.

The patient made a complete recovery. Her depression lifted in the next month to six weeks.

A Penarth GP

I T IS DIFFICULT TO believe, but I had lived in Cardiff and the vicinity for almost nine years without having visited Penarth. My work brought me in contact with its inhabitants, friendly and ordinary folk. The fact that I would spend most of my life living and working there had never crossed my mind, but after meeting my future practice partner, I asked my friends what kind of place was Penarth. Most of them said that it was a pleasant district to live in, with many facilities for sport of all kinds, two sailing clubs, a famous golf club, a bowls club, two tennis clubs, etc.! At that time, the rugby club was famous, and it invited the Barbarians every Good Friday, and the team stayed in a hotel on the prom before it got burnt down.

However, one friend said, "You are going to meet the snobs", and told me that many wealthy people lived there, having made their money from ships and coal. In fact, Marine Parade was nicknamed Millionaires' Row!

On the 1st February 1960, I started work as a GP in the surgery situated in the middle of the town, opposite the library. One of the partners, Dr Bassett, gave me a map of the streets, a list to visit, a prescription pad and off I went on my first round of patients as a GP.

My very first patient was a delightful teacher, Thelma Williams, living in Grove Terrace. She was unable to speak due to a severe sore throat. With a high temperature, she was ordered to stay in bed, given a script for penicillin and told to see me when better, to return to work. On my retirement, thirty-four years later, there was a card from Thelma, my first patient. That was the kind of relationship that existed in those days in general practice – nobody was a number!

I enjoyed the work, which I found easy after so much specialised hospital work. However, there was a heavy workload with long hours, caring for patients night and day.

I made it a golden rule to show an interest in everyone, and to examine them despite the condition appearing obvious, and not just give them a prescription without telling them the diagnosis. Healing or improving a condition is very often due to the attention given the patient and their subsequent faith in the doctor. Respecting a patient always improves their morale.

My old friend Byron Evans told me before leaving the hospital that the biggest luck I could have would be to meet one or two patients that others had failed to diagnose and cure them. Their praise and my reputation would last forever. As it happened, there were two miraculous cures within two months of my becoming a GP in Penarth.

My first patient, whom I saw after a fortnight in the town, was Mrs Hilda Graham, of 47 Redlands Avenue, one of a group of 'prefabs', built during the Second World War. There was just one floor, with a lounge, bedroom, kitchen and bathroom, and the rent was low. Dr Bassett asked me to visit her, saying that neither he nor the senior partner Dr Eastby could make the diagnosis. I remembered Byron's words and off I went, determined that this was my chance.

Hilda Graham was 56 years old, in bed, with her husband caring for her, and she had been unwell for a month. Her symptoms were weakness, tiredness and some shortness of breath even when doing small tasks, such as going to the toilet or dusting her two rooms. There was mental deterioration and depression, although she had been a person who was always full of fun and laughter. Her tongue was sore with a burning feeling, and she had pins and needles in her fingers and toes. I suspected some kind of anaemia, maybe the pernicious type.

On my request, she removed her pyjamas with her husband's aid, and I examined her. Starting with the head, her hair was white, she had blue eyes and she obviously was anaemic. In the mouth, the tongue was red, smooth and shiny. Down to the tummy. I found an enlarged spleen, but no lumps. I asked Mr Graham for a hatpin, and he gave me one about three inches long. She was frightened and asked, "What are you going to do with that?" I explained that it was to test sensation that was absent up to her knees and elbows.

By now the diagnosis was obvious – pernicious anaemia. The anaemia is due to a deficiency of Vitamin B12 and the treatment is injections of the vitamin into the muscle, frequent to start with, until the level of haemoglobin reaches 100 per cent, and then monthly.

I phoned Byron and told him, and he took her into Llandough Hospital to confirm the diagnosis and teach the students. Her blood when she entered the ward was 35 per cent. After a month, she was discharged, and lived until she was eighty, dying of a heart condition – nothing to do with her anaemia.

The second patient was a baby born in November 1959, living in 23 Pill Street, Cogan, on the outskirts of Penarth, towards Cardiff. Cogan people were a friendly crowd and always made the most of the doctor when he or she visited the area. By the time I would come out of my patient's house, there would be another five people on their doorsteps asking my advice – the partners back in the surgery would think I had found a new girlfriend because of all the time I had taken for one visit! It is in Cogan that I saw the last woollen shawl being used to nurse an infant, other than when I would visit the Brecon Beacons with the family on a Sunday in the summer and see several people on their doorsteps enjoying the warmth of the morning sun.

The baby's name was Lynn Miller, a red-haired infant, who had been born at home, attended to by the midwife only, with a normal delivery. From the beginning, she had a cough without obvious cause, and no runny nose or other signs of infection. Both partners had seen her without finding an abnormality. The parents felt she had bronchitis, but despite having been given antibiotics, she was no better.

It was March, and I was asked to visit. Here was another challenge and taking a good history was imperative. Sitting next to Mrs Miller, I listened intently, and the main fact was that the cough had been there since birth. Examination came next, with no visible or external clues. Out came the stethoscope and, as usual, I listened first to the heart. This revealed a most unusual noise. Having been brought up on a farm, it sounded to me like those big threshing machines for separating the corn seed from the straw – what we call in paediatrics, a 'machinery murmur'.

When the baby is in the womb before birth, the oxygen it needs comes from the mother via the placenta or afterbirth, through the umbilical cord, with no use being made of the lungs. A special blood vessel called the *ductus arteriosus* allows the baby's blood to by-pass the lung system until the moment it is born when, with its first few breaths, this vessel closes and the oxygen from then on is received from the lungs. This had not happened with Lynn, and the vessel had remained open, a condition called *patent ductus arteriosus*.

I admitted her to Llandough Hospital the same day, where the diagnosis was confirmed, with every medical student in Cardiff listening to Lynn's heart. The famous Hugh Harley, chest and heart surgeon at Sully Hospital, operated on her, which meant tying an indestructible 'string' around the artery, which would be there forever. All was a success, and the cough disappeared overnight, with the news spreading around Cogan and the rest of Penarth of Lynn's cure and the new young doctor. Where is Lynn now? Nursing in Llandough Hospital, married with two children.

I went to visit John and Hilary Miller, Lynn's parents, at their home, now at 36 Willow Close, when writing this book, when they told me she was their third child, the previous one having died in Sully Hospital – of what? *Patent ductus arteriosus*. I doubt if another family in the world have had two babies with this same condition.

Both these cases, Mrs Graham and Lynn, were of great help for the patients to have faith in the new doctor.

I had been in Penarth for four months when I was called

to a house where the occupant was trying to hang himself. He had a rope around his neck and was ready to tie it to a big hook on the ceiling. He was difficult to control and I asked the police to assist. They took him to Whitchurch Psychiatric Hospital, because he was very depressed. It may be incredible to believe today, but an attempt at suicide then was considered a crime and the patient when better had to appear before the magistrates. This was 1960 – why did it take so long for the law to be changed? I successfully defended him in court. How could he be punished for suffering from an illness?

While I waited my turn in court, a girl of seventeen was in the witness box, having had a child with the accused father in the dock, who denied it. DNA was not heard of in those days, and the chairperson of the magistrates, Miss Kate Davies, asked her "What colour hair did he have"? I will never forget her answer, "I don't know. He didn't remove his hat."

Kate Davies later became my first private patient. When chatting one day, she told me of a very sad episode in her life. She had been educated privately at Malvern Girls' College, near Worcester, when in 1919, the major flu pandemic spread over Europe. There were seven girls sleeping in the same dormitory and they were all sent home. When it was safe to re-open the school, it was only Kate Davies that returned, the other six, all her close friends, had died, at thirteen. More people died of flu in 1919 than soldiers killed during the two world wars.

These statistics show how deadly influenza can be. History tells us of so many epidemics. In south Cardiganshire there was scarlet fever during the nineteenth century, which killed children mostly. Large families were the order of the day and as many as eight, nine or ten out of a family of twelve or thirteen would die within days of each other.

This infection is caused by a germ called *streptococcus*, which produces a poison or toxin that probably kills the patient. What is interesting is that its severity has decreased over the last 150 years to the point of no longer being lethal, even without using penicillin which it responds to. In fact, the illness is now called *scarletina*. It is the only germ that has done this. Why? We don't know. It must be a genetic change, that is, a mutation. I wish more germs did the same, especially viruses which modern medicines have little effect on.

The Miracle Cure

THE PRACTICE IN PENARTH was open on a Saturday night until the end of 1959, giving workmen who could not get there during the week the opportunity to see their doctor.

Two delightful characters frequented the surgery every Saturday night. The waiting room was warm with a lovely gas fire and a fifteen-minute chat with the doctor was free, as were tablets such as aspirin, etc. Money was not plentiful, and the two characters lived two doors from each other in Paget Road in houses built in the old days for dock workers, overlooking the docks. Alice Tonkin, somewhat overweight, lived in no. 6, and Annie Hicks, much thinner, lived in no. 8. Indeed, walking down town, they looked very much like a female version of Laurel and Hardy. Alice would do the talking and Annie would just say, "Yes, yes". The time came to end the Saturday night surgery, and Alice was heard asking Annie, "What shall we do now that the surgery won't be open?" Annie replied, "Yes, what shall we do now on a Saturday night"?

Both were very fond of children and organised bus trips in the summer for their own children and others in the same age group in the area, mainly Paget and Queen's Roads. Later, bus trips were organised for the grandchildren. Favourite destinations were Porthcawl, Bristol Zoo and Bridgewater Fair, amongst others – a day to remember for all concerned.

There was a large rat population in the docks at this time. I saw them myself when visiting patients, foraging for food even in broad daylight. Alice and Annie's sons used to go down with their traps, set them in the evening and next morning inspect the catch. They would destroy them or, if not badly injured, set them free and watch the dogs they had brought with them chase, catch and kill them. The next operation would be to cut off their tails, take them to West House, the council offices in Stanwell Road, where they would be given a few pence for each one. This was the council's method of rat eradication before the employment of pest officers. Pocket money for the lads!

My first visit to the docks area was to the Marine Buildings, at the bottom of the hill going down from Paget Terrace. It was used over the years by customs and excise, and was also where the ships' captains came to report their arrival and where the workers were paid. It is now a posh restaurant. Upstairs, in a single room, on his own, was a retired Norwegian merchant seaman, around 80 years old, who had settled in Penarth. He had a problem down below, with a bag of fluid collecting recurrently in his private area, known medically as a hydrocele.

I was armed with my instruments of torture, a trocar and cannula, and I didn't use any local anaesthetic. The tools had to be sterilised by boiling them in a saucepan; this was done while he was 'sterilising' the area with lots of Lifebuoy soap and water in the far corner. Standing up, so that the fluid would drain quicker, in goes the pointed trocar. After entry, the trocar would be removed, leaving the cannula to serve its function as a pipe to allow drainage. Not a word was said, no groan from the patient, but after almost filling a bowl held underneath, he would say, "I think that's it".

This was a monthly procedure. He did not want surgery to remove the sac. Tragically, the last time I went to visit him there was no "Come in" when I knocked on his door. On entering the dark room, I found him on the floor, stone cold and he had been dead for a couple of days. He died, as he had spent his last years of life, alone. In his wallet, where I obtained his full name for his death certificate, was £1,000 in £20 notes, which was handed to the police. He was a lovely man.

In addition to the tragic events there were comic incidents. I will never forget, in those early days, a woman of sixty-five coming to the surgery with pain in her left foot, at the base of the big toe. Unsure if it was gout or arthritis, I asked to see the other side. As she bent down to undo her laces she said, "I'm sorry Doc, this one is dirty and smelly. I didn't think you would want to see the right one"!

A fortnight before the surgery closed for good, a recently purchased carpet for the waiting room disappeared while the doctor was in his room with another patient. It was a mixed population in those days, from the wealthy down to the poor, as indeed were many other towns in south Wales.

What made general practice interesting was the variation in the conditions and diseases, some bordering on the miraculous. The next story certainly falls into that category. In September 1960, I was sent to one of the nicer houses in Redlands Road. It was to see a woman in her forties who was suffering from diarrhoea. I knocked on the door and her mother greeted me, a lady of about seventy. She seemed thrilled that I had come, and not one of my two partners.

Enid had suffered from looseness of the bowels since she was 11 years old, when she started at Stanwell Grammar School. She had lost four years of schooling due to her condition, which had now deteriorated.

Over the years, local doctors, including consultants at Llandough Hospital, had failed to cure her. When she was 18 years old, the most important gastro-enterologist of his time, Sir Francis Avery-Jones, practicing in London, the Middlesex Hospital and physician to the Royal family, was asked to come to Penarth to see her. He arrived by train in his morning suit and silk top hat, and came by taxi from Cardiff station to her home. He spent an hour with her and suggested different foods, etc., but all to no avail. Everybody was disappointed, especially her father when he received the substantial bill!

I was at a loss as to what to do, but felt that some, if not all, of her condition was in the mind, as her illness had started at a crucial time in her life when she had moved from primary to secondary school. I decided that the best approach was to win her confidence and make sure that she had faith in her new doctor. I prescribed a very old fashioned medicine, known as 'Mist.Kaolin and Morph', a mixture of Kaolin and tincture of Morphia which quietens the bowel and eases any pain. I told her that this was the stuff I had used to cure very many patients, and that I was confident that it would cure her condition.

It is difficult to believe, but before finishing the bottle, taking a dose four times a day, her diarrhoea was gone and never returned. What is the explanation? I am confident that it was her faith in me as a young new doctor and my magic potion that did the trick.

The story does not end there. After the magical cure no other doctor was allowed near her. If she were ill when I was on holiday, she would await my return, however unwell she was. After her mother died, she was lonely and I was asked, in the old-fashioned way, to join her for tea, especially for special occasions like her birthday and Christmas.

As she got older, her vision deteriorated, and nearing her eighties, I would notice the number of cobwebs increasing on the ceiling, with the inhabitants taking a walk when I was there, some reaching the floor. Other unwelcome visitors dressed in their black and blue also came, making themselves at home in the sugar or jam pot – bluebottle flies. I used to try and whisk them away, but the noise they made in their flight excited the spiders, all coming to the front doors of their nests hoping a fly would land on the web and provide a feast. Spiders are usually active at night, but with Enid, it was night and day. The flies they were eating made the spiders very big, indeed some on the carpet looked like crabs on the beach!

Dear Enid insisted I had tea, but the cups were not as clean as they used to be, with brown rings on the inside. To avoid drinking from them, I always sat next to a flowerpot, preferably with a plant inside, and when Enid looked the other way, I would pour my tea into the flowerpot. Before leaving, I would suggest the plant needed water, and took it out to the kitchen, emptying the tea into the sink and replacing it with fresh water.

Enid would insist that I eat her homemade cakes, but with

her hands not as clean as they should be, I kept a plastic bag in a pocket, and Enid's homemade cakes discreetly went into the plastic bag in my pocket and not to my stomach!

I can remember a morning towards the end of her life. She had bronchitis and was confined to bed. When I called as usual, the home help had already been and made scrambled egg for her breakfast, but due to her poor eyesight, half the egg was on her pyjama jacket. At the time, I was caring for my son Ian's young golden labrador, 'Honey'. Ian had gone on holiday, and I took the dog with me to see Enid. Enid was thrilled to see my four legged friend, but when Honey saw the feast awaiting her on Enid's pyjamas, she jumped on the bed and licked it all off. What did Enid say? "I think she likes me", not realising that it was the food Honey was interested in!

After she died, her solicitor came to see me. Enid had left me her house and contents. I had spent many an hour with her, trying to comfort her and lift her spirits, but never realised that she appreciated the attention and care I had given her so much.

MY OWN BREAKDOWN

IN 1968, AT THE age of thirty-four, when all was going well for me in my work as a GP, I became seriously ill.

I suffered a mental breakdown. These were the darkest days of my life, and I write about these experiences here in the hope that they will be of some comfort and help to others who suffer such an experience.

I had been working harder than usual and the long hours had taken their toll on me physically and mentally. When the summer holidays came I was glad of the chance to relax with my family and catch up on lost sleep. However, I found that I could not relax, and returned to work feeling tired. After two weeks back at work, I developed physical symptoms in the form of stomach pain, and thought it was a duodenal ulcer, and was admitted to Llandough Hospital. I was given a barium meal test and it was normal. Failing to find the cause of the pain only made me more anxious. Being a doctor, I knew of all the possible things that could be wrong with me. My worries increased and I could not sleep at night. I could not eat and I was losing weight.

Mental illness often hides itself behind physical symptoms and this was true in my case. People often complain of 'missed heartbeats' and all the doctors' tests, such as ECG, have to be performed to prove to the patient that there is nothing wrong with them physically. Mental stress also hides behind stomach pain and the doctor is tricked into thinking that this is caused by an ulcer or colitis.

The symptoms of stress disorder are anxiety, feeling nervous, tense, agitated, trembling, cold or hot flushes, anger, unable to settle or concentrate, difficulty sleeping, tiredness, overreacting to minor problems, headaches, muscle tension, awareness of heart beating, giddiness, difficulty breathing, nausea, even vomiting. As time went on, I was getting less and less sleep and getting more and more anxious.

After two weeks of hell, Dr Myrddin Evans, a psychiatrist, was called. I poured out my burden of anxiety. I related to him the story of my life and told him of the bitter experiences of my childhood. He listened to me for an hour. He then said confidently, "I think I know what's wrong with you." His words lifted a weight from my shoulders. However, the anxiety continued and pouring it all out did not cure me of the hell I was in – being extremely agitated and tense, unable to concentrate and unable to sleep.

After three days, I was begging to be put out of my agony. Dr Myrddin Evans realised that my mind needed a rest, and I was taken to a single room in a quiet part of the hospital. There was only one answer to my problem: to put me to sleep for a long time in order to give my tortured mind a rest.

I can remember the morning vividly. It was 11 o' clock in the morning and I was given sleeping pills. They had no effect on me, so after an hour I was given an injection of morphine. I woke up three weeks later, having been asleep for twenty-one days and had been given sleeping pills constantly with excellent nursing care attending to my body functions during this time. I had lost four stone in weight and gone down from my usual 13 stone to 9 stone. My hair was turning grey and I was so weak that I could hardly stand.

The pain in my stomach was gone but I was still a sick man with a long, long way to go before being well again. I had to relearn how to live. I was given excellent nursing care and physiotherapy to strengthen my wasted muscles.

However, my mind was far from well. Mental illness is a black hole that is very difficult to climb out of. I felt I was in a deep dry well, going round and round in its bottom, looking for a way out, with no ladder to climb nor rope to cling to. I felt very guilty that I had let myself get into such a state, and that I was causing the doctors and nurses and my family such problems and work.

Dr Myrddin Evans was a brilliant psychiatrist, but unfortunately I became completely dependent on him and clung to him because I was afraid I could not cope without him. One weekend he had to go away to Nottingham, and knowing of my dependence on him he was almost afraid to tell me. He spent time with me every day and I poured out my problems, and wrongdoings from the past. One Friday evening, he had called to see me at the end of the day and after hearing me go on endlessly about the same old things for an hour he said in the end, "Can I go home now?" He was trying to push me back to being self reliant and not dependent on him.

I was in a terrible mental state and frightened to do anything. I had lost confidence in myself to do ordinary tasks. I was frightened even to walk upstairs. There were twenty steps between the ground floor and the first floor, and I was able to manage only a few to begin with. Reaching halfway was a major achievement. After much effort, I reached the first floor, and then walked the 200-yard corridor from one end to the other, usually on a Sunday evening when all the visitors had gone home. My guilt and fear made me anti-social and I was afraid of seeing, meeting and talking to people.

Various methods were used to treat me. One method was distraction – getting my mind away from dark and anxious thoughts. This was achieved by using earphones to listen to classical music. I knew that Rachmaninov, the Russian composer, had gone through a similar illness and that a psychiatrist named Dahl had cured him. In appreciation of Dahl's work, he composed his second piano concerto and dedicated it to him. This was the nearest I could get to someone who had gone through a similar experience to my own. I listened to his second piano concerto scores of times, and in the end it became a conditioned reflex for me to play Rachmaninov whenever I was feeling bad and I felt better after hearing the first few bars. It certainly helped my recovery.

The mountains of the mind are more difficult to climb than any real mountain. Gerard Manley Hopkins has described the hell and despair of mental illness well when he said:

> Oh, the mind, mind has mountains,
> Cliffs of fall, frightful sheer,
> No man fathomed. Hold them cheap
> May who ne'er hung there.

In order to build up my self-confidence, Dr Myrddin Evans told me to write on a piece of paper any statements or sentences that, when spoken or read, lifted me, even if only temporarily. If someone said, "You are looking better today", "Your eyes look brighter" or "Your hair is getting back to its curly state", I would write it down and read it again later. Reading these when I was on my own was very helpful and helped to banish negative thoughts and feelings. I can remember one such saying which I wrote down having a great effect on me, "When you get out in that car and drive to Barry for a walk on the sands, it will do you a world of good."

I began to try and piece myself together again. I found that a tense mind and muscle tension go together. It was important for my body to be relaxed. I used two methods of relaxing myself. One was controlling my breathing. A healthy person does not think about automatic body movements like breathing, but when we are tense our breathing becomes shallow using the upper chest only which causes a lack of oxygen and increases the pulse rate. To relax, it is necessary to breathe deeply, using the movement of the diaphragm up and down and not the chest muscles. This results in pushing the tummy muscles out. I often used this method of breathing in order to go to sleep – all I had to do was continue breathing in this way until sleep took over.

I still use deep breathing in this way to relax myself in a stressful situation, for example while driving. I would advise you to put your hand on your tummy in order to feel your tummy going up and down. A relaxed body is a relaxed mind.

My worst moment was when Jo, my wife, and my two sons, Marc aged 7 and Ian aged 5, were allowed to visit me on a Sunday morning. I found seeing them very difficult, and I was perspiring with a rapid heart rate from the stress of the occasion. When they left I felt completely exhausted.

When the time came for me to go home I had been in hospital for two months. Dr Evans and his staff had done all they could and I knew that the rest of the recovery was up to me.

Dr Evans continued to visit me at home and when he thought I was up to it I would visit him at the hospital to try and get me used to coping in the outside world. One day on my visit to the clinic, I parked my car in the car park outside. I was approached by a man who said that I had driven over his bus. I later found out that he was an inmate, quite harmless, who was once a bus driver who spent his days carrying a stick two feet long around with him. This was his bus, and he pretended to drive it around the hospital grounds, and would park it here and there. I had parked over his stick. Meeting him made me realise how lucky I was and that my illness was temporary compared with the tragedy of this poor man.

Even when I was recovering there were some bad days. This was often when I experienced flashbacks to traumatic events. My childhood experiences came to me often and were most disturbing. These painful events were suppressed and buried deep in the mind, but experiencing them again was a form of relief and a way of getting better.

When I was recovering, I developed an appreciation of the wonders of nature. Even the fresh air, which we take for granted, was a wonder to me. A country walk, a night sky were all new wonders to me. I derived great pleasure in watching my children enjoying simple things and marvelled at their interaction with each other. It was like been born again to a world full of surprises and delights.

I did not go back to work until May 1969, having been off work for seven months. I found the battle to will myself to go back to work very hard. With the help of my wife Jo, family and friends I started enjoying meeting people again. I developed the resolve to get back to help others as I myself had been helped.

I found my first day back very difficult and had to walk out after two hours. However, after a ten-minute walk and with grit, determination and thoughts of my family I went back to the surgery and it never happened again.

I still suffered the occasional panic attack. The panic would come out of the blue and catch me unawares. The physical symptoms of a panic attack were palpitations, giddiness, faintness, chest pains, etc. These decreased as time went by, but they were proof that the healing of my mind was not complete.

I shall be eternally grateful to Dr Myrddin Evans for returning me after a mental breakdown to being a normal human being. He is one of those doctors who will give their time and knowledge tirelessly and endlessly to help their fellow men. His huge compassion was the key to his greatness.

Looking back over this dark period of my life I realise how indebted I am to my wife for being by my side through all the hard times. She has been a tower of strength to me. Thank you Jo for everything.

INHERITED ILLNESSES

M ANY OF MY PATIENTS had heartbreaking diseases, sometimes involving more than one member of a family. These diseases were usually genetic in origin.

One of the duties of the practice was to care for children in Erw'r Delyn School for the physically handicapped, serving south Wales. I remember well three brothers from Senghenydd in the Rhondda valleys, in the late 1960s, suffering from progressive muscular dystrophy. Their names were David, Anthony and Mark Pritchard. The illness causes the child's muscles to deteriorate slowly from the age of three years, and the child usually dies when around fifteen after spending most of their lives in a wheelchair. After David and Anthony died, Mark never smiled, knowing what the future held for him. Life can be so cruel.

Girls don't suffer from the disease, but they carry it and pass it on through their genes. In Great Britain, 30,000 people suffer from such conditions. Research in the last few months has shown that dogs suffering from a similar illness improve with stem cell therapy. Professor Cossu, of the University of Milan, found that dogs with the weakening muscles who are hardly able to walk at 5 months old, can, having undergone this treatment, run around as well as a normal dog when a year old. There is much debate about using stem cells from the embryo, but in this instance, it was blood from an adult dog that was used. We look forward to the day when medical advances can cure tragic illnesses such as muscular dystrophy.

As a GP, knowledge of the patient's family medical history is helpful in making the correct diagnosis, because many illnesses are inherited or genetic. One example in Penarth was the Lane family. I met Nancy Lane on the surgical unit when working with Professor Lambert Rogers on Llanbradach Ward in 1956. She was in the far bed on the left, next to the window, suffering from pain in her tummy. Her X-ray showed gallstones, but she did not wish to have them removed.

When I came to Penarth, the Lane family became my patients. Bert, her husband, had a fruit and vegetable shop, having started his business with a horse and cart, going around the town. The horse was named Tommy, and it was a very small horse only fourteen hands high, and Ken, their son, used to jump on its back when it was in the stable. Ken was once found fast asleep still mounted on Tommy's back. He was a wise horse, and knew the route well, going from house to house. When he went down past the golf club, near the old cement works one day, the horse knew it was the last house to visit. As soon as he heard Bert say goodbye, he was off, back to the stables, but this time, Bert had said goodbye before jumping on the cart. Tommy was gone and Bert had to walk home. Twenty minutes later, he found Tommy back in the yard.

Nancy came to the surgery to see me one day and complained that the pain was getting worse. She agreed to an operation and this was arranged. After five minutes under the anaesthetic and having just begun the operation, her heart stopped. She was only 48 years old. I felt sad. She had become a friend, and if I hadn't told her to have the operation, she might have lived for many years, despite being in pain.

The post mortem was inconclusive. The coronary arteries were normal, but the cause of death on the certificate was coronary thrombosis, despite no evidence of it. I felt very dissatisfied with the verdict.

Bert kept the shop going for many years, and as a family, we bought all our food there. He was a kind man and the children received a bag of sweets or a banana on each visit.

Their son, Ken, lived in Plassey Street. In 1991, at the age of fifty-five, he developed heart problems, and was short of breath even when in bed at night. There was no angina. I sent him to Llandough Hospital four times, and to the University Hospital of Wales three times, to try to get the correct diagnosis. There was much difference of opinion, but one afternoon, he deteriorated and was unable to breathe with a very rapid heartbeat. He was sent to Harefield Hospital as an emergency, where Sir Magdi Yacoub worked. Yacoub decided Ken needed an urgent heart transplant, which he performed himself the next morning, the 4th February 1992. Ken received the organ of a 47-year-old woman who had died of a brain haemorrhage.

Studying the diseased heart after removal, Sir Magdi Yacoub concluded that the muscles were deteriorating to the point where death was imminent. He diagnosed cardiomyopathy, a heart condition genetically transmitted from one generation to the next. It was also concluded that Ken's mother had died of the same condition.

Recovery was complete, but Ken had to receive a daily amount of medication to prevent rejection. This presents its own problems, as it can cause damage to the kidneys, which, unfortunately, happened in Ken's case. He went into renal failure in 2002, but was treated with dialysis. He had a kidney transplant in 2003. He is one of the few people in Britain to have received two different organs by transplant. He had also developed gallstones, and he had his gall bladder removed in 1999 – another family condition.

Ken called to see me when he heard I was writing this book and was not surprised to hear that his history was included. Ken is now 73 years old and very well, enjoying life. By today, we are beginning a new way of treating these genetic illnesses, by ridding the body of the abnormal gene, which will help the patient and, of course, future generations.

During my thirty-four years in general practice, many different diseases came my way. I remember one particular case in a woman of eighty-two, who lived in Mathew Terrace, Eastbrook, on the way to Dinas Powys. She was a widow, and her next-door neighbour had not seen her for four days and, having a key for emergencies, like all good neighbours, decided to enter her house. The woman was in bed, extremely ill. I was called from evening surgery at about 6 p.m. and diagnosed pneumonia and that she was too ill to be moved to hospital.

At the bottom of the stairs, the neighbour was waiting for me, and we entered the lounge where she kept a parrot. All was quiet, and a look in the birdcage revealed that the parrot was dead. I then realised that my patient had psittacosis. A blood test of the patient followed, and proved that it was so. How could the bird have caught the condition? It had no outside contact. I can only think that it had carried the infection all its life and as it reached old age, its defence against illnesses had weakened and the bacteria had taken over. The lady had obviously caught it from the bird. Many illnesses are transferable from animal to human; the latest causing a stir is the bird flu, which can cause a pandemic.

The sad case of a 5-year-old child with tetanus comes to my mind often. This was the 1960s, and she had gone to stay with a school friend for the weekend while her parents went away. On the Saturday morning she fell, cutting her knee, and needed stitches. Not knowing who her doctor was, the adults took her to their own doctor, who cleaned and sutured the wound, but did not give an anti-tetanus injection, nor told them she should come to see me on the Monday to have this done. The district nurse took the ligatures out on the Friday.

Ten days after her injury, on the Tuesday, an urgent call came from the child's mother. She could not open her mouth. She was bundled into my car and was in Llandough Hospital children's ward within twenty minutes, where a tracheotomy was performed to help her breathe and a tube inserted into the stomach via the nose to feed her. Medical students were summoned to assist in twenty-four hour care, alternating with the nurses. I saw her every week for two months, but she died suddenly. It was all so tragic, after a prolonged effort. Today, immunisation against tetanus is routine, and so important.

Alcoholism was common in the area as in many other places across Britain. One patient stands out. I was called one night because the relatives had been unable to control the drunken man who had become aggressive. When he saw me, his doctor, enter the room he became even more aggressive. "Out you go", were his words and, frankly, I was glad to obey because I knew that he intended me harm. I closed the substantial door behind me, and then heard an almighty crash. He had bulldozed his way through the closed door and collapsed on the floor, with his body form left on the woodwork, having felt nothing. The police were called and locked him up in the local police station until he sobered up by the next day.

Whenever I would see an alcoholic, male or female, who usually denied the condition, I knew that bottles would be hidden all round the house, and the favourite hiding place for a gin or whisky bottle was in the toilet cistern!

Undoubtedly, human weaknesses cause a major expense to the National Health Service. If we did not drink excessively, over eat or smoked the dreaded tobacco weed, the country would be several billions of pounds better off, and everyone would live a longer and healthier life.

A Brave Patient

WHEN MY THIRTY-FOUR YEARS of working in the practice came to an end, our list of patients was almost 10,000, having started with half that in 1960. During this time, I saw much suffering but also I saw, as the poet Idris Davies has said, 'the bravery of the simple, faithful folk'. I shall never cease to admire and wonder at the bravery of people in the face of sickness and death. Janet stands out as one the bravest that helped all who cared for her.

Janet was born in a village in north Pembrokeshire in 1944, and she went to Cardigan Grammar School. At the age of fifteen she started working in Lloyds Bank. In 1967, she and her husband moved to Newport, Monmouthshire. Whilst decorating their new house, often until two or three in the morning, Janet became unwell with pain in her limbs to the point that she could not even lift crockery to put back in the cupboards. Her legs were also affected.

Visiting her GP, she was told, "The best thing you can do is ride a bike"! Her right hip was most painful, and the leg seemed to be shortening. Revisiting, blood tests showed she had rheumatoid arthritis, and had damaged the hip by excessive exercise. Cortisone was new at the time, and it was prescribed for her.

She moved house again and came to Sully in 1971. Alun, her husband, heard of the Welsh-speaking doctor in Penarth, and Janet arrived with her incredible history. In fact, I took her records home with me to study them. Here was a young woman of twenty-seven, having already suffered more than most people do in a lifetime.

My first move was to send her to Harley Street in London, to see Dr Dudley Hart, then one of Britain's top rheumatologists. He couldn't do much, but told her she would end up having a right hip replacement, but not for thirty years. By then, she would be fifty-seven. She returned broken-hearted, and I had to re-think. At this time, Mr John Charnley (later Sir) was doing pioneering operations in Whittington Hospital, near Wigan. He had devised a new hip joint and I made an appointment for her to see him. She entered his consulting room where there were eight other orthopaedic surgeons from Britain and abroad, all learning from the expert. After X-rays, etc., he felt she was not psychologically prepared for the ordeal, and she had broken down with tears streaming down her cheeks when talking to him. He also felt that she was very young, only twenty-eight, for such a major procedure. His advice was to wait a year.

She came back to see me. I sent her to two local experts in Cardiff, a rheumatologist and an orthopaedic surgeon, who wanted to fuse the right hip, making it immobile but pain-free. I refused to accept this advice. By now, she was having her second child, the previous being born two years before.

A year later, it was time to return to see Mr John Charnley, hoping that he had more experience of dealing with younger people, including Janet. A similar interview and X-rays were followed by a decision that put a smile on Janet's face. Sir John said he would do the right hip replacement, and after a year's waiting, notification arrived with the Christmas cards.

Ten days after her admission on 15th January 1975, the operation was a big success. When she arrived home on the 4th February on two walking sticks she was pain free. Separation from her family for the first time ever had been painful but worth it. Within weeks, she was walking normally, and she had her third child in 1980.

Janet has suffered from pain in virtually every joint over the years, and by 1992 the left hip had to be replaced by Sir John Charnley's successor.

Major surgery was performed on the right ankle in 1995, and an artificial left shoulder joint inserted in 1997. Janet wears a gold ring on every finger, and she is convinced that they help alleviate the pain, as the fingers with gold rings on since the beginning are much less painful than the others. This seems to prove that a copper or gold bracelet alleviates joint pain.

Janet has undergone fifteen major operations during her lifetime.

She is a very dynamic person, and has worked endlessly for the Arthritis Research Council, collecting £100,000 for the cause, and awarded their gold medal for her efforts. The money has been raised by organising all kinds of charity events, fashion shows, handicraft, cookery demonstrations, coffee mornings, bingo, lectures, flag selling – anything that brings in the money.

Her greatest and bravest effort, however, was in 2001, when she walked the London Marathon course, four or five miles a day and completed it in six days. For a woman of fifty-seven who had undergone fifteen major operations, including two artificial hips, walking twenty-six miles is incredible. When her GP saw her photograph in the local paper, he called to ask her who had given her permission – nobody had asked him!

Janet's artificial right hip is now 32 years old, and she is grateful that I did not agree to fusion. She can do everything without trouble, and she lives a full life. She is an inspiration to all those suffering from arthritis, and shows the triumph of the human spirit rising above adversity.

THE SLEEPLESS MAN

S LEEP, IN ALL FORMS of animal and human life, is fundamental. Indeed, sleep takes up about a third of our lives. That is, if we live to be seventy-five, we will have slept for twenty-five of those years.

We all have our personal sleep needs, which vary from seven to nine hours. If we are deprived of sleep we feel horrible, mentally tired and unable to perform complex tasks. That is why doctors working long hours are a danger to their patients. When I was doing my first caesarian operation, after twenty-four hours continuous work and the registrar saying "Get on with it", I had no choice. However, all workers deprived of sleep are a danger to themselves and others.

Apart from long working hours, there are disorders that interfere with the normal pattern of sleep. Sleep deprivation is unfortunately deliberately used as a torture and to extract confessions.

Alan Guppy came to see me in the surgery in 1972 and told me that he could only sleep for two hours, then he would wake up and be unable to go back to sleep. During one fortnight, he had not slept at all. When he lay in bed his mind was overactive, but he denied that he had any problems, marital or otherwise. He just could not switch off. He would go to bed at midnight and get up before 7 a.m. After his short sleep he would just lie there.

Examination and tests revealed no abnormality, and he was not depressed. I prescribed all kinds of sleeping tablets, even big doses of anti-depressants but to no avail – he just could not sleep.

Having tried all kinds of medications, I referred him to the Cardiff Sleep Clinic. He stayed in the clinic overnight with his head wired to a machine that recorded electrical activity of the brain. Natural sleep records a special pattern, but the machine showed that he had no such pattern, and he was told they could not help him. I then sent him to the London Sleep Clinic, but the test gave the same result. He came back in despair.

One day, he saw an advert in the paper of a therapist in Barry who claimed to be able to relax people, and help with sleeping difficulties. The therapist certainly relaxed him with self-hypnosis, but he did not sleep. In fact, she was so successful at relaxing him that, after leaving her house, he was told to walk a quarter or half a mile before driving home in order to 'wake up' properly. In a hurry one day, he jumped in the car without walking a quarter of a mile and at the first traffic lights he came to he went straight through the red, luckily without an accident or killing anybody.

He has been unable to find any cure for his sleeplessness, and he now gets strong sleeping pills from his GP, which give him two hours 'sleep' and he is remarkably normal the next day.

I went to see him at his home in Penarth for his permission to write about his case, and he told me of his early years. He developed diphtheria when he was 3 years old, and was admitted to the Merthyr Isolation Hospital for eleven weeks. His voice box had closed, and a hole was made in his windpipe to allow air to enter his lungs, that is a tracheotomy – otherwise he would have died. It is difficult to know whether this was responsible for his condition in one way or another.

Five per cent to ten per cent of those suffering from sleeplessness genuinely cannot sleep, and no cause is ever found. It seems that Alan is one of these sufferers.

Almost every day, there is a road accident, sometimes fatal, and it is estimated that half of these are due to the driver not having slept properly the night before, due to insomnia.

HYPNOSIS

THERE ARE MANY WAYS of curing a patient and a good
doctor will try all avenues. One that is ignored too often is
hypnosis. No two patients are the same, even though suffering
from the same disease; their personality and constitution are
different. One's ability to treat patients depended on their
personalities and physical make up. So it is with hypnosis –
some respond easily, others do not respond at all.

It would be difficult to find a more controversial subject
in the history of medicine than hypnosis. Unfortunately,
when the profession shied away from its use, it got into the
hands of amateurs and entertainers, with its ensuing bad
name. However, in the 1950s, this all changed with the law
on hypnosis restricting its use on stage, etc., followed later
that year by the British Medical Association agreeing to its
use professionally for dentistry, medicine, obstetrics, etc.

What is hypnosis? Essentially, it is a state of mind induced
in one person by another, in which suggestions are readily
accepted and acted upon more powerfully than when awake.
Put simply, the hypnotised person's mind is more open to
suggestion.

You would be very surprised how easy it is to hypnotise. I
learnt the art at Cardiff University in 1981, when the British
Society of Hypnosis held a weekend course there. Having
thought about it for years, I decided to go to the course. It was
an undoubted success and I felt ready to start when and where
necessary.

Next day, back in the health centre, I told my receptionists
the news that I was now a hypnotist! One of the girls said
immediately that she would like to be my first patient. Pam
Jones told me she wanted to stop smoking because it was
damaging her health and also that she could not afford it. She
was 45 years old and had worked with me for twenty years,

smoking 20 cigarettes a day. Here was my chance but if I failed, everyone would know!

When she finished work one afternoon during that week, we went to a quiet, unoccupied room. I adopted an impersonal, but professional attitude because I knew her so well. I was able to catch her attention easily, and within seconds she was hypnotised. I couldn't believe it – I had hypnotised my first patient! In this state, the patient can hear every word that is spoken and is able to do whatever is asked of them.

I deepened the trance state using a method I had been taught the previous Sunday. I then said all that was necessary for her to stop smoking, followed by 'awakening'. It had taken only ten minutes, and she was pleased. A further two or three sessions were necessary to complete the course. The next day, her smoking was down from twenty cigarettes to three, and after two more sessions, she smoked no more. She has not smoked since.

Her coughing stopped almost immediately and, when I met her the other day for permission to include her name in this book, she estimated that she had saved between £10,000 and £15,000.

Hypnosis is so easy in teenage girls. A patient came to the surgery one day, accompanied by her mother. Her complaint was of continuous sneezing, every twenty seconds or so. It all started when the young girl was sitting in the front row in the chemistry laboratory in Howell's School, Cardiff. The teacher was demonstrating the preparation of chlorine, which she inhaled. After going home, her mother was worried, and rang the surgery and I gave them an urgent appointment. When she arrived, not knowing what else to do, I tried hypnosis. Within minutes, it was all over. The girl was hypnotised in her mother's presence and, with suggestion, the sneezing stopped, never to return after regaining consciousness. They both went home feeling very pleased.

The following day, I was in the Marks and Spencer's store in Queen Street, Cardiff, the main floor being about 100 metres long. As I went through the front door, somebody was shouting "Dr Elias, Dr Elias. I'm cured". It was the teenager, with a big hug, followed by a kiss from her mum. Never before or since have I been greeted with such feelings of appreciation in Marks and Spencer's!

Success did not always come my way. While attending a party in Cogan Social Club one evening, with the alcohol flowing, and fish and chips to eat, a chip got stuck in a young woman's throat and she choked and died. It was tragic and affected everyone deeply, especially her best friend who had been sitting next to her. She was distraught and unable to swallow anything, but eventually she managed to drink fluids, and for almost ten years, all her food had to be liquidised. Specialists were consulted, psychologists and psychiatrists – all to no avail. When all other avenues had been tried I offered her hypnosis, although I was doubtful if I could succeed because of all the years since the incident.

She went under quite easily but, although I tried everything, I failed to cure her. Speaking to her husband the other day, he said she was now normal and eating everything, even chips! Sometimes time is the only cure.

As I had to belong to the Hypnosis Society that trained me, patients often arrived from a distance. One evening, a couple came from the Rhondda valleys, wanting to stop smoking. The husband said it was impossible for anyone to hypnotise him, and there was no purpose in trying, so his wife popped on the settee, and he was invited to sit the other end of the room to observe proceedings. She was hypnotised relatively easily, and the next stage was to deepen the 'sleep' using arm elevation, the right arm resting on the couch in a horizontal position and rising on my suggestion without effort. I looked around to see how he was and, to my astonishment, he was deeply asleep. His wife's arm was six inches from the resting position but his was directly upright. Never say you cannot be hypnotised!

One evening, I visited my friend, Professor John Dodge and his wife Mary. We were both students together. His daughter, Catherine, known as Kate, was 13 years old. During the evening the conversation turned to hypnosis. John told me that his daughter Kate had been bullied at school when she was 6 years old. John and Mary did not complain about the matter to the staff, and did not know who the culprit was. Ever since then she had been unhappy and suffered from nightmares. I suggested hypnosis, but he would not believe me that this could work. However, he agreed to try that evening.

Kate went to sleep very easily, and on deepening the trance, I told her that she was going back in age from twelve, eleven, ten, etc., to six, known as regression. Speaking to her, she would reply as she spoke when she was a 6-year-old. I then gave her a piece of paper and a pencil, and asked her to write her name. She did, in bold childish handwriting, again like a 6-year-old. Next, she told me who was sitting next to her in school, and told me her name. Both parents had forgotten who this person was but remembered when she told us. I mentioned the bullying and she became agitated and very disturbed. She named the bully, and gave the full story of this unfortunate period in her life. Gradually, after talking it through, she calmed down.

Next came the process of bringing her back to being thirteen again. She returned to consciousness with a big smile. John and Mary phoned me a month later to say that Kate was much happier and that the nightmares had disappeared.

My experiences with hypnosis have proved to me that it has its place in medical practice, that it is not something for entertainment on a stage, and if someone needs treatment for a condition that responds to hypnotherapy, I would advise giving it a try.

VITAMIN D – THE WONDER VITAMIN

AFTER RETIRING I STILL study medical papers and books and feel that I should stress the importance of one wonder vitamin – Vitamin D. It is only recently that we have realised its importance in all aspects of our physical and mental health.

When I was a student, I remember reading about rickets caused by lack of this vitamin that became prevalent when people moved from the countryside to large polluted cities to work indoors in factories with reduced exposure to sunlight. It affected children mostly, causing skeletal deformities and weakness in bones and muscles.

There are two sources of vitamin D. First, it is manufactured in the skin when exposed to sunlight; then enters the bloodstream and is distributed throughout the body. Because of our northern latitude with long winters and short summers it means that for six months of the year our body is making very little vitamin D.

However, there is no need for the dangerous practice of long hours of sunbathing, which can cause skin cancer. We produce enough vitamin D if our face and arms are exposed naturally to the sun for an hour during a week. It is important to remember that a 70-year-old makes less than 25 per cent vitamin D compared with a 20-year-old exposed to sunlight for the same length of time.

The second source is food. It occurs naturally in oily fish, such as mackerel, sardines, tuna and herring, and also in eggs, liver and milk. During the Second World War the government ordered vitamin D to be added to margarine.

I have always preached 'breast is best' for babies, but breast milk contains very little of the vitamin, and with the rapid growth of a baby's bones in the first and second years a supplement is certainly recommended. Many countries put vitamin D in powdered milk, bread, breakfast cereal and margarine. It helps maintain healthy bones. A deficiency of the vitamin produces thinning of the bones, which leads to fractures, pain and deformities.

My brother Elwyn, a professor of medicine, always tells his students about an event in Glasgow in the middle of the last century. Situated in the north of the country, and with smog prevalent, there had been very little sunshine for months. In the early summer, the local Sunday schools had a bus trip to the seaside. It was a lovely sunny day. The children bathed in the sea and played on the beach in the sun, and unknown to them they were making large amounts of vitamin D in their skin. Arriving back home in the evening, several of them developed muscle spasms and pain – a condition called tetany. The explanation was that the vitamin D had mobilised the calcium from their blood to the bones in their body, which had been deficient in vitamin D. This lowered the level of calcium in the blood and the muscles produced the spasms!

Vitamin D improves muscle strength, which reduces the falls and fractures in the elderly. Falls are the single most common cause of injury in the elderly and account for 40 per cent of all nursing home admissions. In 2009, researchers in Manchester University enrolled ninety-nine adolescent girls between twelve and fourteen. Blood levels of vitamin D were measured as well as their muscle power. Those without vitamin deficiency performed significantly better in exercise tests.

Vitamin D helps our body fight infections. People with deficiency are three times more prone to influenza and colds in the winter. In fact, it has been called 'the antibiotic vitamin'. The cells of the immune system, called T cells, are not able to fight off serious infections in the body without adequate quantities of the vitamin.

It helps prevent diabetes, types 1 and 2. There is a link between low levels of vitamin D and type 1 diabetes later in life. Children in Finland are more than a hundred times more likely to develop type 1 diabetes than children in sunny Venezuela! Children given supplements of vitamin D are a third less likely to develop diabetes. I am not saying that vitamin D is the sole factor in these statistics, and we must remember that other factors such as genetics play their part. Similarly, with type 2 diabetes associated with the elderly, low levels of vitamin D mean higher incidence of the disease.

It has anti-cancer properties also, and can help prevent cancer of the breast, bowel, ovary and prostate. Recent studies show that low levels of vitamin D are associated with a 25 per cent increase in the incidence of breast cancer, and a 15 per cent increase in deaths.

My biggest surprise is that the frequency of multiple sclerosis in the population correlates to the latitude we live in. Higher than thirty-seven degrees where there is less sunlight exposure increases the risk of multiple sclerosis by 100 per cent. Statistics from Australia are almost beyond belief – the risk in Tasmania at the southern end is five fold that of the sunnier Queensland in the north. Taking 10 mcg (micrograms) a day is able to reduce the risk of MS by 40 per cent. For people already suffering from the disease, it has been found that a high level of vitamin D decreases the relapse rate.

Vitamin D and the mind. The vitamin D is beneficial in healing depression – both of the unipolar and bipolar kind. There are suggestions that it has a positive effect on dementia and Alzheimer's disease. It is definitely beneficial for the skin – wound healing, atopic dermatitis and psoriasis.

Deficiency in vitamin D is associated with increase in body fat. It is soluble in fat, and some will disappear into the tissues and becomes unavailable for use to perform its many functions.

We can only come to the conclusion that certain groups would benefit from vitamin D supplementation – children under five, the over fifties, vegetarians who don't eat oily fish, housebound people and multiple sclerosis sufferers.

However, before you start dosing yourself with cod liver oil I would like to quote two proverbs – 'Moderation in all things' and 'You can have too much of a good thing'. Too much vitamin

D is harmful. The sensible dosage recommended for children is 5 mcg, 10 mcg for adults and 15 mcg for those over seventy. The best advice is to always consult your doctor regarding the dosage before taking any vitamin supplements.

EUTHANASIA

T HE JOURNEY OF LIFE has a beginning and an end. I have mentioned more than once the joys of delivering parcels of happiness to different families, that is, assisting with the first journey from the womb to the outside world. If there is a difficulty, rules apply to cope with all eventualities, which are adhered to, having been taught to us as students and since.

But, may I mention the omega, death. We received no lectures on the subject in medical school. Consultants do not see the process of bereavement in its entirety, and it is the family doctor who deals with it most often. As a GP, I came to look on the patients as friends and enjoyed their company, even the humblest of them taught me about life and their deaths caused considerable pain and distress to me as their doctor.

This dilemma of dealing with a patient's death has followed me throughout my life and trying to ease the pain of their last days without crossing the line and helping them to die with dignity. Maybe a doctor hardens to a degree, but never enough to avoid being disturbed by the request of a patient to be put out of their misery. I have never helped a patient die, although I have been asked to do so many times. I suspect, however, that many doctors have, out of pity and compassion, given too much morphia in these situations.

Two patients come to mind that caused me much anxiety. The first, a woman of seventy, who was living in Bristol and suffering from leukaemia, which was untreatable at the time. Her sister lived in Penarth, and was a patient of mine. Despite having grown apart over the years, my patient felt the least she could do was offer to care for her terminally ill sister. Her sister accepted. After three months, a phone call came asking me to visit, at 6.55 p.m. on a Thursday evening, with surgery closing at 7.00 p.m. I called on the way home. My patient said that her sister was extremely ill, bedridden and did not want to stay alive. I decided to go to the bedroom on my own, and there was the sick patient, as white as the sheet she was lying on, finding difficulty in speaking, yet fully conscious and in control of her senses.

I sat at her bedside and talked to her. Our discussion went on and on, and by the end I wasn't sure which of the two wanted to 'end it all'. She would not live for more than a few days, but circumstances had reached a critical stage and I wondered whether I should interfere? There were three ways of dealing with the problem. The first was, I could give her a sleeping tablet to help her sleep that night and then return the next morning to re-examine the situation. Secondly, a small amount of morphia given by injection, to quieten the mind but not enough to kill. The third choice was to give enough morphia to kill. If a hundred GPs were faced with the problem, it would be interesting how many would follow which procedure.

What did I do? I took the middle road, and gave the patient enough morphia for her to sleep, but not to kill her, and I went back the next morning to re-assess the situation, having slept all night with a clear conscience.

The other case was a patient and friend, a man of fifty, suffering from a slowly progressive disease of the central nervous system. This was during my final year at the practice. He was also depressed, which was understandable. After retiring, I was pleased to spend some time with him every month or so – he had moved to the Cardiff area and had a new GP so my visits were purely social. His illness went on for years and by 2002, he could not move arm or leg, and needed twenty-four hour care. Spells had been spent in a hospital for chronic neurological diseases, but eventually he became fed up with them. His intellect was unimpaired. The year 2002 was when euthanasia became legal in Holland, allowing two doctors to examine the patient and if both agreed, one was allowed to perform the act if the patient requested it. We discussed this possibility more than once, but could not agree what to do.

Suddenly one day, I heard that he had gone to the continent and there could only be one reason for his visit. He was cremated there and his ashes brought back and I was present at the ceremony when his ashes were scattered on the River Wye, where he had spent happy days fishing.

Should we change the law in this country? It will eventually become statute, as happened with abortions. Until then, we have to abstain from the temptations of giving in to the demands of the patient and stay out of the country's jails.

I have walked the streets of Penarth in my mind since starting this chapter, and there are at least twenty patients that spring to mind who had requested me to perform euthanasia. Much time would be spent sitting on the bedside with each one, discussing the pros and cons. It was not only the physical pain that made them ask, but also the mental suffering, depression, etc. The relationship between husband and wife was important. If the love that brought the couple together was still evident, every second together was important, and these people rarely, if ever, asked.

It is a complex problem, very much in the public debate and it is difficult to please everybody. It is the doctor's conscience that rules many a decision.

A DOCTOR ON HOLIDAY

CRUISING HAS BEEN MY vacation of choice, especially when the children became old enough to come with us. It all started in 1971, on the old *Canberra*, creaking its way up and down Biscay.

My experiences on holiday have been varied and interesting, sometimes hilarious. I normally say, when I am on holiday and asked what my work is, that I am a window cleaner. If you tell people that you are a doctor you are constantly pestered by people seeking advice. When sitting at a table of six or eight, and not knowing the others until we sit down for meals, the variation of people one meets is endless. Discussion is continuous after getting to know each other, and if the world of medicine is mentioned, I shy away and say I know nothing about it, and that my specialty is a bucket of water and a rag – not much can be said about that!

It was in the 1980s, on *Canberra*, and I was having lunch when a woman of ninety-three passed out on the table next to us. I could not leave her there with her head bent forwards and unconscious. Up I got, put her flat on the floor, loosened all her garments, and started resuscitation. She was pulseless. I took out her teeth, grabbed her nostrils and started blowing into her lungs, and at the same time thumped her chest. She had so much lipstick on that I looked like a clown! However, her eyelids flickered – she was alive, and gradually regained consciousness. Amazingly, in the evening, she was on the dance floor. There she was, stepping briskly. Incredible. She was so grateful.

When I got back to our table, there was much discussion about the miracle and I had to confess that I wasn't a window cleaner. At the table were a lovely Yorkshire couple, Lily and Fred, on their first cruise, celebrating their golden wedding. I was last from the table having been held up, and Fred asked,

"Can I speak to you?" This was the fifth day of our trip and we were off Sicily. Lily had been to see her GP before coming to make sure her health was satisfactory, and that there were no problems for the holiday. She was found to have raised blood pressure and given one tablet a day for this. Being anxious, she was also given sleeping pills, one at night, a black and white one, I remember it well, Dalmane. Fred said Lily had a problem. She was sleeping all day and awake all night. I realised that she was taking the sleeping tablet in the morning and the blood pressure pill at night!

The most fascinating story occurs again on *Canberra*. We were a table of eight, and getting there the first night, we sat down to be joined by a couple that arrived hand in hand, John and Barbara. He was no spring chicken, his hair was dyed and he did his best to be young. She was in her thirties with plenty of paint and powder on her face. She wore a wedding ring, but I couldn't be sure that they were married. In the evening they danced actively.

As the days went by, their relationship seemed to deteriorate, and by the sixth day both were miserable, with nothing much to say. Holding hands had ceased and I could see that there was a problem. Out on deck, the next afternoon, with the ship in port, Barbara had gone on a tour while John was sitting by the swimming pool, reading a book from the library. To be polite, I said "Hello", and he was glad to have a chat.

I confessed I was a doctor and asked him if there was a problem, and that the holiday was to be enjoyed. He poured it all out, that they had met two months previously, he having been a widower for ten years. A whirlwind romance followed, and they were married on the day before sailing. All was well for the first two nights, but his physical prowess had deteriorated to the point of being non-existent. Could I help? I felt sorry for him, and thought what could I do – this was before Viagra was heard of. I told him that I used special pills myself if I was overtired, and that they worked very quickly

– within an hour of taking one – the dose being one a day. I fetched the pills from my cabin and I told him not to tell Barbara. He was very grateful. They were there for dinner, but after that we did not see them for three days. Getting worried, I passed their cabin, and on the door was the sign, 'Do not disturb', with a tray of food, with the plates empty, outside their door.

After three days, they surfaced, and came down for the evening meal holding hands with beaming smiles and talking away. He gave me a wink, did not mention the pills, but next day told me how fantastic they had been. Could I please get a supply to take home or tell him what the pills were? Their honeymoon continued in true honeymoon style and when we parted after breakfast on the disembarking morning, he gave me a cheque for £50 for saving his marriage.

The pills were junior aspirin. I had brought them with me in case the children had a temperature, sore throat or earache. Another example of the effect the mind has on the body!

LIFE SAVING AT A PETROL STATION

THE SAYING, "ONCE A doctor, always a doctor" is very true. In an emergency in the Penarth area someone always seems to remember that I have been a doctor and ask my help or advice.

One day after I retired, I was getting petrol in Cogan when, going to the kiosk to pay, one of the girls at the cash desk was shouting "Dr Elias, Dr Elias, come quick, we have a man who's desperately ill!"

The man was fifteen yards away, and I went to his aid immediately and recognised him as one of my former patients. He was in his car and was very ill, looking ghastly with a pulse rate of 250 beats per minute. I knew from experience that he would not survive very long in this condition. An emergency phone call was made for an ambulance. I realised that the ambulance would take time to come and that I had to try to keep him alive until it arrived. I knew that if he sat up, he would lose consciousness and if he was flat, he would be gasping for breath, so I kept him at an angle of 45°, and talked to him all the time.

When he got to hospital, the ECGs showed ventricular fibrillation, and it is only 2 per cent that survive in this state outside hospital. He was later fitted with a pacemaker that switches itself on if this condition recurs, and was an in-patient for a month. He is now well, and grateful for my intervention and for the excellent care at the hospital.

A few days after the incident, to my amazement, the story appeared in the *Sun*, the *Daily Mirror* and on the internet with the man's wife, Mrs Ballett, describing Colin's recovery as a miracle, especially after the desperate moments at the petrol station. It was front-page news in the *Penarth Times*, filling most of the page, with his photograph and a report.

ITV were keen to include the 'miracle' in their news

bulletin, and while I was writing this book in my study upstairs, sitting by the window, I saw a reporter I recognized coming up the drive with his two black bags ready to record his interview. By this time I was tired of all the publicity. Opening the window, I asked, "Can I help you?"

"Are you Dr Elias?" he asked.

"No", was my reply. "I live in the upper half of the house, and he lives on the ground floor and has gone to his native Cardiganshire for a week's break." He disappeared down the drive, and I didn't hear any more from him.

DISCOVERING SOMETHING NEW

AFTER RETIRING THERE IS no peace and quiet for a doctor – someone always turns up asking for advice. Sometimes, however, looking into such cases leads one to find something completely new – which cannot be found in the medical textbooks.

Throughout this book, I have written about the effect of the mind on the body. Perhaps there is not a better example of this than a condition that causes a sensation of burning in the mouth, which can extend up to the nose or/and down towards the stomach. Strangely, two old friends, both ex-patients, knocked on my door with this symptom. The opening words of the conversation being, as usual, "I hope you don't mind"! I couldn't turn them away.

Examination revealed no physical abnormality. However, examining their mental state provided the answer. They were both depressed. Various local medications of the mouth had been tried, to no avail. The only answer was anti-depressants. After a month, there was considerable improvement in their moods and their mouths, and after another course of pills, all was back to normal.

I researched the condition and found the answer thanks to my dentist friend and neighbour, Hywel, who lent me his dental bible. Sure enough, the condition was described there after I had failed to find it in my medical textbooks – Burning Mouth Syndrome.

THE IMPORTANCE OF HOBBIES

WILLIAM JAMES, THE PSYCHOLOGIST, preached the gospel of relaxation, saying that it is important for man's well-being, mind and body. I have found this to be true, and would advise everybody to keep a balance in their lives between work and relaxation.

The most important thing about a hobby is that it absorbs the mind totally, and makes one forget work and life's problems. Maybe you think that sitting down doing nothing is better, but the tendency then is for the mind to wander and for worries to come to mind, which means that one is no longer relaxing.

Fishing

My initial knowledge of any form of fishing came from my father who described how he and his siblings went tickling trout in a stream that flowed through their land at Glanhirwen, their smallholding. The technique is interesting. The hand is placed gently, palm down, on the surface of the water and kept there until it achieves the temperature of the river. Often the trout would come to investigate, and could be caught easily. If not, the hand would be lowered towards the riverbed until the fingertips felt a fish. It was then grabbed and brought to the bank.

I was sceptical of it all until one day when fishing on the Cwerchyr, a tributary of the famous Teifi, a couple of lads – sons of the mill at Pwllcornol – showed us how and brought up ten trout within minutes. This was where it all started for me, the river being about two metres wide and heavy rain was necessary to turn the water cloudy or even muddy. This would allow the fish to see the bait, usually a worm, without seeing us.

A life-long friend of mine, Ricey, always came with me. My rod was a small branch from a tree, attached to a piece of nylon string, two or three feet long with a hook on the end, holding a worm, dangling in the water. We learnt quickly that pools, usually below a faster stretch of water, were the most productive. This was heaven for two young lads, forgetting everything; time meant nothing. Always competing against each other, it was my luck one afternoon to catch two fish. Arriving home on the farm, I knew my Aunty Lisa enjoyed eating fish, but she was so annoyed with my late arrival that she refused them. Next day, I took them down to the butcher's shop in Llandysul where David Lewis gave me half a crown for them.

Following my success on the Cwerchyr, I mentioned it to my school friends. One of them asked, "Were you using jam?" This was the first I had heard of it, but I soon learnt more about this infamous bait. It is made from the eggs of the female salmon, usually milked from her by hand – how else? There are two methods of use: the first is to put an egg on a hook as it is. Secondly, warm the eggs in a saucepan, like making jam – which is where the name comes from – using a wooden spoon, until it is stiff-like paste. Into a jam pot, put the lid on and it is ready for use. I must confess being given some once by a cousin from Beulah, no name mentioned! The hook is dipped in the jam, then a worm attached, down into the water and the pool soon boils with activity, with fish arriving from a distance once they taste the feast from lower down river. This was strictly illegal of course, and against a true fisherman's instinct.

In my thirties, I became interested in salmon fishing, and I joined Llandysul Fishing Club. This is where the Hardy family, makers of the best fishing rods, etc., came in the early part of the twentieth century for their holidays, staying at the Porth Hotel, the proprietress also owning four miles of the river from Llandysul North.

My first experience was at Easter, around 1973, with

my two sons, 10 and 8 years old at the time. A licence was essential, meaning a call at Sergeant Jones's shoe shop in Lincoln Street. Off to the riverside about 2.00 p.m., but no fish were caught until about 5.00 p.m when there was a huge pull on the line whilst in Jack's Pool. It was obvious, even to a beginner like me, that a salmon had been enticed to swallow my bait, a 2-inch minnow, brown in colour. To my surprise, it came in quite easily and before I saw it, I was afraid that it might be a knackered old fish, having been upstream to breed and somehow survived to spend the winter in the river. These are called 'spent' fish.

I went back to see the sergeant and showed him my catch. He could not believe it, the only salmon caught in that part of the river that day. He checked the fish's eyes, thinking it must have been blind, but no, and then showed me three sea lice on the fish's skin, proving that it had recently come from the sea, as these parasites die in fresh water within three or four days. It was my first salmon, 8 lbs in weight, and I was hooked for life, with the same thrill now as forty years ago when at the river bank.

My days in practice meant meeting thousands of people, and one of my patients was a lady of ninety, Mrs Fowler, who lived in the Plymouth Nursing Home. Her son, Bill, Cardiff's best-known auctioneer, came to see me when her condition was deteriorating. This was our first meeting, and chatting as always, he told me of his mile stretch of the river Usk, which he owned, on Pantygoytre Farm, three miles below Abergavenny. He invited me to join him when fishing, and there was no need to ask twice. We have enjoyed wonderful days together in the peace and tranquillity of his riverbank, and I learnt so much from him about fishing and nature in general. His biggest catch over the years in this stretch was 36 lbs. Bill's photograph, with the fish, appeared in the *South Wales Echo* and *Western Mail*. I still have a copy.

I am sad to say that Bill is no longer with us, and the mile of the Usk has been sold. All I have are memories of a kind man, a true friend, a wonderful fisherman and the happiest of hours we spent on the riverbank.

I once saw a very sad scene on a stretch of river where two swans lived. Nesting annually, they pair for life. The hen had been poisoned by lead pellets used by fishermen to weigh down the bait and take it to the river bed where the fish normally feed. This causes muscle weakness and, unable to hold her neck vertical, gradually the head would drop into the water, causing drowning. There was the cob, trying desperately to hold her head above the surface. It brought tears to my eyes. A year later, the cob was on his own, miserable, with feathers having lost their shine and cleanliness. It was the last time I saw him.

Gardening

The best place to use our five senses is undoubtedly the garden. First, Vision: Walk past a floral border of different colours and shapes in early summer in places like Powis Castle or the Botanic Garden near Carmarthen. Attracting wildlife adds to the view, for example, butterflies flock to a buddleia or Michaelmas daisy. What about a nesting box for birds, for instance the blue tit, or feeding them with seeds and nuts?

Secondly, Smell: Recent research has shown that smell acts on the emotions more than any other sense, and can raise the mood almost instantly. A garden without perfume is only half a garden! There are numerous plants that fall into this category: roses, lilies, jasmine, etc., my favourites being daphne odora or daphne bholua. Some years ago, I was in the Valley of Kings in Egypt viewing the crypt of a king that had died 2,600 years BC. On the wall, there was a carving of his queen smelling a flower. This is the first depiction of perfume I know of. The Egyptians grow hundreds of acres of jasmine south of Cairo, to collect the petals and squeeze the oils from them to sell in expensive bottles. By today, it is possible to extract the chemicals from the petals and re-create the mixture in the laboratory. The companies that sell these artificial perfumes place wires over the purchaser's head, that is, an electroencephalograph, or EEG, and find out by the recordings made what the person responds to the most. On the way out, he or she can purchase that perfume, ready in a few minutes, whilst the flower in the garden has spent years growing and developing it!

Hearing: Most, if not all of us, enjoy some form of music but who can resist the dawn choir, or a song thrush producing about twenty different tunes. Some enjoy the sound of flowing water, either over stones in the garden, or a fountain.

Taste: Fruit and vegetables, eating them fresh without chemicals added by growers. I needn't say more.

Touch: I was surprised at the amount of pleasure touching various trees and shrubs gives. One of my unexpected joys was seeing a blind person putting his hand on the trunks of *acers* in a famous garden centre: their names, *acer griseum*, *acer pensylvaticum* and *acer serrula*. When you next go to an established garden centre, ask them have they any of these three growing there and try it out. Close your eyes. You will be rewarded.

Yes, gardening has been one of life's major joys, and by observing carefully, something new every day. As old age arrives, a few pots around the house may be sufficient with, of course, one under the bed! I learned about these pleasures when I was a youngster on the farm. The garden was about forty metres square, near the farmyard, with a plentiful supply of natural manure to make it productive – indeed, all the vegetables came from it. Friends often arrived in the evenings. It was our social contact, and in the summer they would be asked to visit our 'Eden'. Looking back on this time, I am sure there was an element of competition, unofficially of course, as to who had the best garden.

When I was 10 years old, I was given my own square metre, a packet of lettuce seeds and shown how to get on with it. They were easy to grow, and it was a joy seeing the little rows filling and turning green.

After serving my apprenticeship, the time had come to assist with the main garden. My unforgettable memory is of an old apple tree, probably 50 years old, that fruited on one side one year and the opposite the next. I have learnt of apple trees fruiting every other year, but not one half one year, and then the other the following year.

The years in college and studies prevented much thought of gardens. Moving to Penarth changed all this, with the purchase of a house and garden, but when working the soil, the telephone often disturbed me with someone ill and needing a visit. Also, the next-door neighbours glad to see Doc having a break, and would want a chat. Eventually in 1971, the right house and garden came on the market, doctors having lived there for sixty years, and a quarter of an acre garden. Purchasing was a must, the fences being so high.

I was in seclusion, not that I am a loner, but after days, even weeks of being with people, night and day, it was important to get away. Exercise was necessary, and where better than in my heaven, doing what I had when in school and on the farm, digging and shovelling earth or manure. The mind would disconnect from patients, and with the exercise and fresh air, I felt much better afterwards.

The garden was redesigned with a large greenhouse to hold a vine, Black Hamburgh, similar to that in Hampton Court, with its roots down to the River Thames, 100 metres away, and selling over 200 tons of grapes annually to the public, with one person caring for it full-time throughout the year. We had a new patio facing south, making the most of the sunshine, a lawn for the lads to play on and a fruit cage to grow strawberries, tayberries, raspberries, etc. and prevent the birds from getting most of the crop.

Thirty-six years have elapsed since my move. It has been a joy, but it is time to look for a smaller house and garden.

It will be a sad rift, but it comes to us all. I should mention a lovely playroom in the back of the house, overlooking the garden, about 20 metres square, where thirty Penarth ladies came every day during the Second World War to knit clothing for members of the armed forces: gloves, socks, balaclavas, etc. It is an historical building.

Music

Music has been an essential part of my life. My first memory of being thrilled by what I heard was at a concert in my chapel in west Wales, given when a local lad was leaving to serve in the armed forces during the Second World War. A collection was made, and the proceeds given to the departing person. Entertainment was provided by local talent, and there was plenty of it.

Cardiff is an excellent centre for classical music, including St David's Hall and, later, the Millennium Centre. Sir Charles Mackerras was a patient of mine for years, living in Penarth, always arriving outside my consulting room door with earphones on and a CD player on his lap, not saying a word until he entered my room.

The greatest was Bryn Terfel, living then in Railway House, a residence on its own by the line from Cardiff to Penarth, where he could sing his heart out and not be heard. He came to the surgery one afternoon when I'd recently acquired a new computer that took some getting used to. "Next, please", I called, and after entering, and me looking at the screen in front of me, I asked "Name?"

"B T Jones", was the reply – who else but Bryn. Confirmed when I saw him, large in physique, and larger still in his reputation but so humble in his attitude. Isn't that how the best people are? It was an honour to care for him and his family during their stay in the area: the greatest bass-baritone in the world, and the most likeable. It has been one of life's thrills to listen to him on so many occasions.

Siblings

My brothers and sister have formed a very important part of my life, despite being brought up apart. Their scholastic and other successes have meant so much to me. The more I think about it, the more tragic it is that we were separated.

Hefin, eighteen months my junior, was a very capable sportsman when young. He played in the Aberystwyth Football Team and competed in the Welsh League, this on Saturday afternoons having already played rugby for Ardwyn Grammar School in the morning. An athlete, he won the Victor Ludorum for the best pupil, also the Cross Country Championship three years in a row. The London School of Economics was his first college, and after graduating there, he went to University of Wales, Bangor to study theology, gaining his BD and then a scholarship to Oxford University for three years. This is when he married Ceinwen. He became head of religious studies at the University of Glamorgan, and still preaches every Sunday.

The twins, Dyfed and Dilys next, four years younger than myself. Dyfed played football for the under-19s for Wales four times. Invited to join Aston Villa, he reached the second team but saw no security there at the time, and transferred to Hereford United, then in the Southern League. They allowed him to study for his A levels at the local technical college, gaining three As after a year, and went to University of Wales Swansea to study economics and history. After gaining his degree, who was chasing him but Ron Greenwood, manager of West Ham United, offering him a full-time position in football. He refused, and went to teach in Essex, joining Romford Football Club. Eventually, he returned to Llandudno as head of economics in John Bright Grammar School, joining 'Boro' United, a famous football team at the time, and made captain. He married Hazel in 1964. Dyfed was Footballer of the Year with Hereford, the same with Romford for two years, and made Best Player in north Wales when he returned.

It was Dilys that gave me the impetus to get this book going. She went to Barry Training College and was a leading light in drama at the college, and continued to enjoy amateur dramatics when she moved to Birmingham to teach, where she met her husband, Wil. The interest continued in north Wales, and she taught in various primary schools until her children arrived. She eventually became head of an assessment school in Anglesey, dealing with children with mental and physical problems.

I had the joy of seeing her ability to interest a child when she happened to be in my house at the same time as my granddaughter, Rhian, from London, then 7 years old. Rhian had never played a note of music, but since spending half an hour with my sister, she has enjoyed the piano every day since and has taught herself the flute. Yes, Dilys did what every teacher should do: kindle a flame that remains alight forever!

What can I say about my little brother Elwyn, having reached the pinnacle of the medical profession with an international reputation! I remember him lecturing in Cairo some years ago, and, a few days later, one of the consultants there had a patient with liver problems he could not deal with. The consultant placed a label around his neck, as the patient couldn't speak English, and wrote on it, 'Dr Elias, England'. He was put on the next plane to Heathrow, and two days later, he came through the door of Elwyn's unit at the Queen Elizabeth Hospital, Birmingham.

There are so many people that owe their lives to him. One is David Griffiths, an able solicitor who practised in Newcastle Emlyn. He had a liver transplant in Birmingham some ten years ago, and a few months later, one of my cousins went to his office to pay for legal services he had rendered. "How much do I owe you?" said John, my cousin. "Nothing" came the answer. "I am indebted to the Elias family for being alive and well."

MEDICINES TO EXTEND LIFE

W HAT ARE THE SECRETS of longevity? One way, but not
pleasant, would be to develop a chronic illness such as
arthritis, which would restrain the person in mind and body,
and look after their physical 'well-being', that is, keep them in
cotton wool, as it were.

There is no doubt that there are tablets or chemicals that
will, if taken regularly, extend life. I will name four, and putting
them in a single tablet would cost less than a pound a day. I'm
surprised that not one of the manufacturers has caught on. It
could add ten years to the final number.

The first is Statin. There are over four million people
taking this daily in Great Britain, the highest number for any
medication. What does it do? It decreases the amount of fat in
the blood stream that furs the arteries, hence less blockages
that cause heart attacks and strokes, also circulation in the
legs.

Secondly, there are vitamins. A mixture of the essential
ones and the correct amount. I remember reading about an
illness in the USA called hypervitaminosis: if a small amount
does you good, a large amount should do you a lot of good.
This is not so, and taking too large a quantity can make you ill.
Vitamin D is perhaps the most important of them all.

Thirdly, there is a chemical that prevents sudden
irregularities of the heartbeat, which can cause sudden death.
A recent one is a 'calcium channel blocker'.

Lastly, there is our old friend, aspirin, which has proved
itself over the years. My Aunty Lisa was one of twelve children,
most of them dying of strokes and heart trouble. She lived to
be eighty-five. Why? She was a migraine sufferer, with two
or three attacks a week. The only pain killer at the time was
aspirin to ease her headaches, but they did something else too,
they thinned the blood and stopped it clotting. It also prevents

cancer of the colon. Today, the advice from nutritionists is to eat more fruit and vegetables, maybe five varieties a day. One of the reasons why they work is that they contain aspirin, and in fruit, the highest concentration is in the seed – no wonder you see so much in breakfast mixtures like muesli. Vegetarians add seeds to many of their dishes.

Perhaps I should mention one other, which will surprise some, chocolate. It naturally contains many chemicals, the most important being phenylethylamine, which is an aphrodisiac and mood elevator. The king of the Aztecs, Montezuma, had numerous wives and the way he kept them happy was by drinking fifty cups of drinking chocolate a day. Of course, it contains cholesterol, but incredibly, it contains antioxidants as well, which counteract its deleterious effect.

THREE WAYS TO STAY HEALTHY

THERE ARE THREE WAYS to stay healthy and help the finances of the health service: avoid overeating, excessive alcohol intake and don't smoke. We would all live longer and feel better throughout our lives. Moderate exercise should be added as a fourth.

Also available from Y Lolfa:

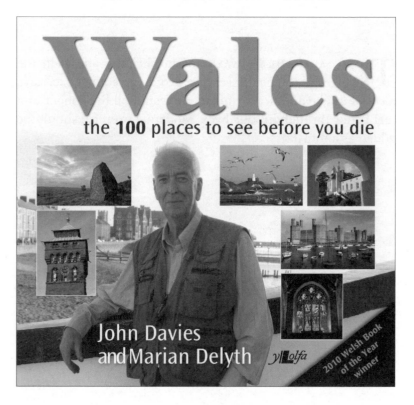

Wales

the **100** places to see before you die

John Davies
and Marian Delyth

y Lolfa

2010 Welsh Book of the Year winner

£29.95

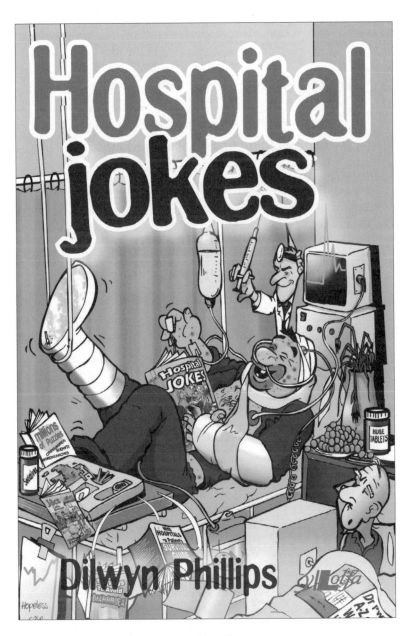

Hospital jokes

Dilwyn Phillips

£3.95

A Doctor's Tale is just one of a whole range
of publications from Y Lolfa. For a full list of
books currently in print, send now for your
free copy of our new full-colour catalogue.
Or simply surf into our website

www.ylolfa.com

for secure on-line ordering.

TALYBONT CEREDIGION CYMRU SY24 5HE
e-mail ylolfa@ylolfa.com
website www.ylolfa.com
phone (01970) 832 304
fax 832 782